D0422074

A NEW OWNER'S
GUIDE TO
GREAT PYRENEES

JG-167

Overleaf: Adult Great Pyrenees owned by June and Laurence St. Onge.

Opposite page: Adult Great Pyrenees owned by Priscilla Marsh.

The Publisher wishes to acknowledge the following owners of the dogs in this book, including: Gale Armstrong, Ruth Baak, Stephen and Mary Berman, Nancy and Larry Carr, Rhonda Dalton, Lorraine Fennemore, Mary Fodness, Theresa Granito, Joan Laguna, James and Kim Lasley, Pricilla Marsh, Christine Palmer-Persen, June and Laurence St. Onge, Laurie Scarpa, Kristina Sodeika-Trinka, Doug Stitt, and Stephanie Wolk.

The author acknowledges the contribution of Judy Iby to the following chapters: Health Care, Sport of Purebred Dogs, Identification and Finding the Lost Dog, Traveling with Your Dog, and Behavior and Canine Communication.

Printed and Distributed by T.F.H. Publications, Inc.
Neptune City, NJ

A NEW OWNER'S GUIDE TO
GREAT PYRENEES

KIM LASLEY

T.F.H. Publications, Inc.
One TFH Plaza
Third and Union Avenues
Neptune City, NJ 07753

This book has been published with the intent to provide accurate and authoritative information in regard to the subject matter within. While every precaution has been taken in preparation of this book, the publisher and author assume no responsibility for errors or omissions. Neither is any liability assumed for damages resulting from the use of the information herein.

ISBN 0-7938-2816-3

Printed and bound in the United States of America

ABOUT THE AUTHOR

Kim Lasley and her Mistry Great Pyrenees live on a sprawling 20-acre ranch in Ramona, CA, situated in the southernmost portion of the state. She shares her life and her love of dogs with her husband, Jim, and 3 young daughters—Krysta, Deanna, and Jayme, ages 7, 4, and 7 months respectively.

The versatile and active family's interests extend well beyond their successful Great Pyrenees breeding program. In addition to operating Kritter Kamp, a large boarding kennel, they maintain a vineyard of wine grapes bottled under their own Mistry Vineyards label, and they house and coordinate a very active Great Pyrenees rescue service.

As though that in itself would not keep any average person busy, Kim has also been one of Southern California's most successful and highly sought after professional dog groomers for over 20 years.

Since 1977, Mistry Great Pyrenees homebreds have won numerous top awards at National and Regional Great Pyrenees Specialty shows. Mistry Kennels bred, owned, and sired dogs have accounted for 41 champions with US, Mexican, Canadian, International, and Hall of Fame titles. For the last 16 years, Kim has worked with Joan Laguna co-owning, breeding, and showing Great Pyrenees.

Kim's purebred dog interests have run the gamut of breeds and have included German Shepherds, Border Collies, and Boxers. In addition to her special love of Great Pyrenees, she has imported, bred, and shown Pyrenean Shepherds. She is a member of the Great Pyrenees Club of America (GPCA) as well as having served on the board of the Great Pyrenees Club of Southern California, which she joined in 1977. Kim has also been a member of the Orange Coast Great Pyrenees Fanciers.

Kim's rescue efforts extend far beyond her work on behalf of the breed in Southern California in that she has also served as National Rescue Coordinator for the GPCA. No dog of any breed escapes her concern. For many years, she has been conducting pet educational programs with her dogs at schools.

Her programs provide instruction on caring, feeding, handling, and grooming of all dogs. The Mistry Great Pyrenees have also been used as mascots for the Special Olympics in the early 1980s, and have been highly successful as therapy dogs at hospitals and convalescent and retirement homes and as livestock guardians.

Eventually, Kim also plans to add judging purebred dogs to her repertoire of talents.

Contents

2001 Edition

The Great Pyrenees has the ability to make friends easily, and he enjoys the company of other pets.

The gentle and fun-loving Great Pyrenees is an ideal companion for children.

With the proper training, the versatile Great Pyrenees can achieve any goal he desires.

The playful nature of the Great Pyrenees makes him a fun playmate for people and other dogs.

The Great Pyrenees' polar bear-like charm is often hard to resist.

All breeds of dog—regardless of size, shape, and color—bear wolf ancestry. Understanding this origin may help dog owners better interpret their pets' behaviors.

HISTORY and Origins of the Great Pyrenees

ANCIENT HISTORY

There are currently over 300 distinct breeds that are officially recognized by the respective purebred dog registries of the world. What comes as a surprise is that all breeds, regardless of size, shape, or color, trace back to a single common ancestor. And what may be even more important in the overall scheme of things is that research reveals that the development of the dog bears a striking parallel to the development of mankind itself.

To fully understand why any given breed looks and acts as it does, one must go back to the dawn of civilization—a time when mankind's major pursuit in life was simply that of survival. Providing food for himself and his family and protecting the members of the tribe from danger were about as much as early man could handle.

During this time, man undoubtedly saw his survival efforts reflected in the habits of one of the beasts of the forest—a beast that made ever-increasing overtures at coexistence. That beast was none other than *Canis lupus*—the wolf. Thus, a relationship based purely on the need to survive had begun. The ages themselves, however, would show this was a kinship that would prove far more beneficial to mankind than one ever could have imagined.

Wolf families had already developed a cooperative and efficient system of hunting for survival. Man was not only able to emulate some of these techniques, but as time passed, he found he was also able to employ the wolves in capturing the animals that would constitute a good part of the human diet.

In turn, wolves saw a source of easily secured food in man's discards. Moving in closer and closer, the more cooperative wolves found they had increasingly less to fear of man. The association grew from there.

THE DOG BREEDS DEVELOP

The road from wolf-in-the-wild to "man's best friend" (*Canis familiaris*) is as long and fascinating as it is fraught with widely varying explanations. There seems to be universal agreement on one thing, however, and that is the wolves' abilities to assist man in satisfying the unending human need for food were the most highly prized.

In *The Natural History of Dogs,* a study of the development of dog breeds, authors Richard and Alice Feinnes classify most dogs as having descended from one of four major groups. Each of these groups traces back to separate and distinct branches of the wolf family. These groups are the Dingo Group, the Greyhound Group, the Northern Group, and the Mastiff Group.

The Dingo Group traces its origin to the Asian wolf (*Canis lupus pallipes*). Two well-known examples of the Dingo Group are the Basenji and, through the admixture of several European breeds, the Rhodesian Ridgeback.

The Greyhound Group descends from a coursing-type relative of the Asian Wolf. The group includes those dogs that hunt by sight and are capable of great speed. The Greyhound, Afghan Hound, Borzoi, and Irish Wolfhound are all examples and are known as the coursing breeds or sighthounds. They are not true hounds in that they do not hunt by scent.

The Arctic or Nordic Group of dogs is a direct descendent of the rugged northern wolf (*Canis lupus*). Included in the many breeds of this group are the Alaskan Malamute, Chow Chow, German Shepherd, the much smaller Welsh Corgi, and Spitz-type dogs.

The fourth classification, and the one we take particular interest in here, is the Mastiff Group, which owes its primary heritage to the rugged Woolly Tibetan wolf (*Canis lupus chanco* or *laniger*). The great diversity of the dogs included in this group indicate they are not entirely of pure blood in that the specific breeds included have characteristics that reveal they have been influenced by descendants of the other three groups. This widely divergent group is known to include many breeds we now classify as sporting dogs, the true hounds (those that hunt by scent) as well as the guard/protection and flock guardian dogs.

It is the ingenuity of man that deserves full credit for the selective process that produced dogs who excelled in some, but not all, of the traits that had been passed down from their lupine ancestors. The undesirable characteristics that could have been inherited were all but nullified. A perfect example of this is seen in how the wolf's territorial instinct, communal spirit, and bravery are reflected in the character and working ability of the Great Pyrenees, which is thought to be one of the oldest breeds of dog in the world.

Great Pyrenees were of great value to the peasant shepherds of Spain and France. The dogs' exceptionally keen eyesight and strong guarding instincts helped the shepherds to protect their flocks from wolves, bears, and even human predators and thieves.

As mankind moved out of the caves and developed a more sophisticated and complex lifestyle, he found he could produce animals that could suit his new and specific needs from these descendants of the wolf. More often than not, this selective process was shaped by how and where man lived.

The herding wolves were selectively bred to retain their rugged constitution and their ability to round up their prey, but the prey instinct itself was, for all intents and purposes, eliminated. From still other descendants of the original wolf stock, man eliminated both the prey and herding instincts in favor of developing their communal and protective qualities. Man did so in order to ensure the safety of his domesticated livestock.

"MAN'S BEST FRIEND" ARRIVES

It is at about this point in history that we can stop calling them canines and start referring to them as *Canis familiaris,* more commonly known as dogs. Particular characteristics were prized, so inbreeding practices were used to both intensify the desired characteristics and eliminate those that opposed the efficiency of the dogs.

When the Mongoloid people migrated westward into Europe, their dogs—Mastiff-type descendants of the rugged Tibetan wolf—went with them. The migrants dispersed themselves throughout the important mountain ranges of Europe, where environment and the specific needs of the people developed their dogs into separate and distinct types.

There are no written records to indicate what blood may have been introduced and combined with these early canine immigrants to produce the flock guardians that followed. However, we do know that these dogs, each in their own distinctive ways, patrolled the flocks throughout the Europe's mountain ranges. Among them we find the Komondor of the

Intelligence, strength, and endurance enabled guarding dogs to carry out their duties efficiently. The Great Pyr's long, heavy coat protected him from the natural elements and made him invulnerable against attack.

Caucasus, Germany's Leonberger, the Kuvasz of Hungary, the Maremmas of the Italian Alps, the Anatolian Shepherd Dog of Turkey's Anatolian Plateau, and the magnificent dogs that lived and worked along the Pyrenees Mountain ranges–the Great Pyrenees.

Remains found in the fossil deposits of the Bronze Age in Europe (1800-1000 BC) bear a striking resemblance to these dogs of the Pyrenees. It is known that the peasant shepherds of Spain and France held the dogs in highest esteem. Without their trusted guardians, the shepherds would have been at a loss to protect the flocks from wolves, bears, and even human marauders and thieves that roamed throughout the mountainous regions.

The dogs that watched over the flocks had a precocious sense of smell and exceptionally keen eyesight. They needed to be tough in every aspect–physically hardy and totally impervious to every natural element inflicted upon them. They had long heavy coats that helped make them invulnerable against attack, and they were armed with broad iron-spiked collars.

It should not be thought that these were purely ferocious brutes, however. These invaluable companions to the shepherds were blessed with courage, intelligence, and devotion of legendary proportions.

There is no wonder that these Pyrenees Mountain dogs were held in such high regard by the men for which they worked. In addition to their courage, the dogs had to be capable of performing the most subtle and complex duties. At times, the dogs lived almost entirely on their own, interacting with the shepherds only for their basic necessities. The dogs lived, slept, ate, and traveled with the sheep and goats, and were accepted as members of the flock. The rugged winter storms often isolated the flocks, so on many occasions the dogs were called on to make the decisions to ensure the well-being of their wards.

When not actually sleeping among their flocks, these shepherd dogs could be found on bluffs where not a single animal would escape their watchful eyes. When the dogs moved about, they did so slowly and quietly to avoid exciting the animals and throwing them into a panic or stampede. When a predator appeared, the placid demeanor of the Pyrenean dogs disappeared. The gentle flock guardian became a raging powerhouse, strong enough to bring down the most fierce or clever adversary.

STATUS SYMBOLS

We find the first written reference to this remarkable breed in 1407 AD, when historian Mons. Bourdet recorded activities surrounding the Chateau of Lourdes in France. Bourdet tells of the Pyrenean dogs used as guards, roaming freely and accompanying the human guards as they proceeded on their rounds of duty. The breed's success and visibility at Lourdes captured the attention of the nobility throughout France. Soon, every large chateau had a Great Pyrenees standing guard.

Early in the 1500s and continuing on for well over 100 years, many of the Pyrenees dogs emigrated from France to Newfoundland with the Biscay fisherman. Their duties were not unlike those that had been assigned to them by the shepherds. They were loved companions that protected the colonists' homes and kept a vigilant eye out for the wild beasts of the island.

The charms of the Pyrenees served the breed well by endearing them to the young Dauphin of France, who later became Louis XVI. In 1675, he was vacationing at Barreges, met one of the dogs there, and took him back to the Louvre. The Pyrenees soon became the court dog of France and created great admiration for the breed. Royalty rose and fell over the following centuries, but the nation's love of the Great Pyrenees never wavered. Even following the revolutions and counter-revolutions, the dogs readily found homes with farmers throughout France, especially with the shepherds in the high Basque Country of Southern France.

In 1907, the Pastoure Club at Lourdes, Hautes Pyrenees, in France was organized. The goal of the club was to create interest in and perpetuate the Great Pyrenees breed. The organization produced the first written standard of the breed, and their efforts assisted in assembling an entry of 53 males for the first known Pyrenean Specialty show. This was the largest number of the breed ever shown together at one time.

Factions, however, restricted any great contributions the Pastoure Club could have made, and it was left to Bernard Senac-Lagrange to create an entirely new club some 20 years later—the Reunion of Pyrenean Dog Fanciers. Senac-Lagrange's first order of business was an official standard for the Great Pyrenees, completed in 1927.

The definitive standard and Senac-Lagrange's concerted efforts brought a degree of uniformity not only to the thinking of those that championed the cause of the Great Pyrenees breed, but also

In the 1400s, Great Pyrenees were used as guard dogs for the Chateau of Lourdes in France. The breed's exceptional work ethic won the admiration of the nobility in France.

to the breed itself. As better specimens were produced, the seeds of the Great Pyrenees as an envied competitor in the show ring had taken root and would rapidly spring forth around the world.

The Great Pyrenees in England

Until the end of the 19th century, no great interest was developed in the breed as a show dog in Great Britain. The first real attempt to establish the Great Pyrenees as a viable breed was made prior to World War I when Lady Sybil Grant developed an interest in the breed.

In 1909, Lady Grant traveled to the Pyrenees Mountains in search of stock to found her Milanollo Kennels. One of the dogs she returned with was registered as Milanollo Patou. Patou took a first prize at The Kennel Club show in London. The win ignited a degree of publicity and captured the first attention of other purebred dog fanciers. No sooner had any genuine interest begun when the devastating effects of World War I made it necessary for Lady Grant to disband her kennel.

Unfortunate circumstances continued to plague the breed. By 1933, there were only 3 Great Pyrenees remaining in all of Great Britain. It was therefore of the utmost significance that Mme.

Jeanne Harper Trois-Fontaines established her De Fontenay Kennel in 1934. In the ensuing years, the De Fontenay Kennel became so strong that it was not only able to withstand the rigors of yet another World War, but became internationally renowned as well.

Immediately upon the end of the war's hostilities, Mme. Harper resumed breeding with such success that De Fontenay dogs were exported to many parts of the world where they helped to establish the breed. Mme. Harper is also credited for having bred England's first homebred champions.

The breed grew over the following decades in Great Britain, culminating in the historic Crufts' Supreme Best in Show award of Mr. and Mrs. F. S. Prince's Bergerie Knur. Knur captured this coveted win over 8,000 dogs at the world-famed show.

THE PYRENEES IN AMERICA

The first Pyrenees came to America in 1824 when General Lafayette sent over a pair of males to his friend J. S. Skinner, editor of *The American Agriculturalist.* He recommended their use as livestock guardians against wolves and sheep-killing dogs, and further predicted they would be of great value to the woolgrowers in the rapidly developing new country.

It was not until 1931 that the first breeding pair of Pyrs was brought to the United States. Mr. and Mrs. Francis V. Crane of Needham, MA, purchased the pair to found their famous Basquaerie Kennel—the first United States registered kennel for the breed.

Subsequently, the Cranes scoured Europe and imported over 50 Great Pyrenees, of which they established a bloodline that would go on to have influence throughout the United States, Canada, Mexico, Puerto Rico, and South America. Their dogs even recrossed the Atlantic to England, Belgium, the Netherlands, and India.

The die had been set. The Crane's efforts and influence assisted the breed to become fully recognized by the American Kennel Club (AKC) in 1933. Again, through the efforts of Mr. and Mrs. Crane, The Great Pyrenees Club of America was founded on December 2, 1934, with Professor Will Monroe as the first president.

Basquaerie Kennels' import, Urdos de Soum, became the first American-crowned champion for the Great Pyrenees. He completed his championship at the Eastern Dog Club show in Boston, MA, in February of 1934.

In 1824, General Lafayette introduced the Great Pyrenees to America. He recommended that the dogs be used as livestock guardians against wolves and sheep-killing dogs and also predicted that they would be very valuable to woolgrowers in the new country.

The Cranes' imported Ch. K'Eros de Guerveeur of Basquaerie, who won the first US all-breed Best in Show at the Eastern States Exposition Dog Show in Springfield, MA, on September 23, 1939.

Since its inception, the membership of the Great Pyrenees Club of America has done its utmost to maintain the character and working ability of the breed. No efforts have been made to make this a popular breed. In 1999, the 3,638 dogs registered with the American Kennel Club placed the Great Pyrenees 45th among the 147 breeds recognized by them. This is a position of respectability, but one in which there is no danger of the breed falling victim to faddists or exploitive breeding practices.

In France, the Great Pyrenees work with the Pyrenean Shepherd, or as they are called in France, *Le Petit Berger.* Pyrenean Shepherds herd the livestock while the Great Pyrenees protect it. In their home country of France, the Great Pyrenees is called *Le Chein de Montagne des Pyrenees*—the Mountain Dog of the Pyrenees. In England and Europe, the breed is known as the Pyrenean Mountain Dog, and in the US, they are known as the Great Pyrenees.

CHARACTERISTICS of the Great Pyrenees

All puppies are cuddly and cute, but Pyr pups are beguiling beyond words. With their adoring eyes, oversized feet, and sheer size, the puppies have a special polar bear charm that is hard to resist. There is nothing more adorable than a litter of Pyr puppies, nestled together and sound asleep, one on top of the other. But in addition to being cute, puppies are living, breathing, mischievous creatures that are entirely dependent on their human owners for *everything* once they leave their mother and littermates. Furthermore, the innocent-appearing, dependent little Pyr puppy that weighs around 20 pounds when you take him home grows quickly, becoming a very large, and somewhat gawky, adolescent.

Buying a dog, especially a Pyr puppy, before you are absolutely sure you want to make that commitment can be a serious mistake. The prospective dog owner must clearly understand the amount of time and work involved in the ownership of any dog. A giant breed, like the Pyr, has all its own special considerations that must be added to those of any standard-sized dog. Failure to understand

"Rosie" and "Bucky" show off the polar bear-like charm that is characteristic of the Great Pyrenees.

When choosing a breed, take into consideration your family and lifestyle. The Great Pyr's protective instinct and gentle nature makes him a great playmate for well-mannered children.

the extent of commitment involved is one of the primary reasons that there are so many canines in animal shelters.

Before anyone contemplates the purchase of a dog, there are some very important conditions that must be considered. One of the first important questions that must be answered is whether or not the person who will ultimately be responsible for the dog's care and well-being actually wants a dog.

If the prospective dog owner lives alone, all he or she needs to do is be sure that there is a strong desire to make the necessary commitment that dog ownership entails. In the case of family households, it is vital that the person who will ultimately be responsible for the dog's care really wants a dog. In the average household, mothers, even working mothers, are most often given the additional responsibility of caring for the family pets. Regardless of the fact that today's mothers are out in the workplace, often they are saddled with the additional chores of feeding and trips to the veterinary hospital with what was supposed to be a family pet.

Pets are a wonderful method of teaching children responsibility, but it should be remembered the enthusiasm that inspires children to promise anything in order to have a new puppy may quickly wane. Who will take care of the puppy once the novelty wears off? Desire to own a dog aside, does the family's lifestyle actually provide for responsible dog ownership? If the entire family is away from home from early morning to late at night, who will provide for all of a puppy's needs? Feeding, exercise, outdoor access, and the like cannot be provided if no one is home.

Another important factor to consider is whether or not the breed of dog is suitable for the person or the family with which he will be living. Some breeds can handle the rough and tumble play of young children while some cannot. On the other hand, breeds the size of the Great Pyrenees are so large and clumsy as puppies that they could unintentionally injure an infant or toddler.

Also, there is the matter of grooming. A luxuriously coated dog is certainly beautiful to behold, but all that hair takes care. In the case of Pyrs, they shed their coats twice a year. Vacuuming daily is a reality when you own a Great Pyrenees.

Remember that the new dog must be taught every household rule that he is to observe. Some dogs catch on more quickly than others, and puppies are just as inclined to forget or disregard lessons as young human children are.

CASE FOR THE PUREBRED DOG

Although all puppies are cute, not all puppies grow up to be particularly attractive adults. What one person considers beautiful is not necessarily attractive to another. It is almost impossible to determine what a mixed-breed puppy will look like as an adult. Nor is it possible to determine if the mixed-breed puppy's temperament is suitable for the person or family who wishes to own him. If the puppy grows up to be too big or too active for the owner, what will happen to him then?

Size and temperament can vary to a degree even within a purebred dog. Still, selective breeding over many generations provides the would-be owner reasonable assurance of what the purebred puppy will look and act like as an adult. Points of attractiveness completely aside, this predictability is more important than one might think.

Choosing a purebred Great Pyrenees puppy provides a good indication of what he will look and act like as an adult.

A person who wants a dog to accompany him on morning jogs or long distance runs is not going to be particularly happy with a lethargic or short-legged breed. Nor is the fastidious housekeeper, whose picture of the ideal dog is one that lies quietly at the feet of his master by the hour and never sheds, going to be particularly happy with a huge shaggy dog or one that has a temperament reminiscent of a hurricane.

Purebred puppies will grow up to look like their adult relatives, and by and large, they will behave pretty much like the rest of their families. Any dog, mixed breed or not, has the potential to be a loving companion. However, a purebred dog offers reasonable assurance that he will not only suit the owner's lifestyle but the person's aesthetic demands as well.

WHO SHOULD OWN A GREAT PYRENEES?

The Great Pyrenees is a multi-purpose dog. He is a wise and dependable working dog. For the family, he fulfills the traditional role as a companion and guardian to adults as well as children. He enjoys participating in whatever the family is doing, and keeps a watchful eye over each member of his family.

A working couple can also make a good home for a Great Pyrenees provided there is outdoor space for the dog when they are away at work. When they are at home, the dog should not be left outside but included, whenever possible, in the evening and weekend activities. A Pyr needs to feel like he is a full-fledged member of the family.

Provisions must be made for the Pyr puppy when the family is away from home. Never leave a puppy or adolescent dog loose and unattended at any time. Youngsters can get bored and, if left alone inside a home or apartment, they may end up chewing or getting into things of which you don't approve. Needless to say, an apartment, condo, or townhouse will make it extremely difficult, if not impossible, to own a Pyr puppy, unless you are home to take him out to walk several times a day.

A securely fenced yard is the best place to keep your Pyr when you are not home. Cyclone fencing is recommended at least 5 to 6 feet high. It is also important to make sure that there are no holes in the fence or gaps between the fence and the ground. If a Pyr can get his head through a gap, he can get

An enclosed outdoor area gives your Great Pyrenees the chance to exercise while keeping him safely confined.

his body through. The Pyr's head can be deceiving. Adults appear to have big heads, but a lot of that size is actually hair. Therefore, they are able to get through holes that would seem to be much too small.

Providing your puppy access to the whole yard is fine, but if you enjoy gardening, flowers, and shrubs, sharing an attractive garden with a puppy that might enjoy doing some gardening on his own is not going to make you happy. A fenced dog run, tucked away on the side of the house or at the end of the garden, is a better idea.

A 10- by 40-foot space is adequate for a run, but larger is better yet. This should be enclosed with fencing of the proper height. Small gravel several inches deep will keep the Pyr clean. A large doghouse located at one end of the run will protect him from the elements. A manger of straw over soft blankets makes a great bed in the doghouse, because most Pyr youngsters like to drag their blankets outdoors.

Some Great Pyrenees owners like to provide water using a "lik-it," which is a special kind of faucet that releases cool, clean water when the dog licks it. This eliminates the constant scrubbing and refilling of a water bucket, and you are secure in the knowledge that your pet always has water available.

CONSIDER SIZE

One of the most frequently asked questions of a Pyr owner is, "How much does a Great Pyrenees weigh?" At maturity, a male stands an average of 27 to 32 inches at the top of the shoulder and weighs approximately 100 to 125 pounds. Numbers for females are lower, but even at that, a Pyr, male or female, makes a commanding presence in your home, as well as in your automobile.

No, you don't have to have a station wagon or mini-van to transport your Pyr, but it's a good idea. A full-grown Pyr occupies the same space as a human member of your family. Despite the appearance that he is an ideal outdoor dog, the Pyr enjoys being with people, indoors and out.

A Great Pyrenees requires a lot of socialization and obedience classes from puppyhood through adolescence. Excursions to the grocery store, the school playground, and the park are all part of your dog becoming a good canine citizen. A Pyr loves to ride in the car, wherever you're going. While he enjoys a long walk, due to his extraordinary size and rapid growth, he must be conditioned slowly and sensibly before he is exposed to vigorous exercise.

CHARACTER OF THE GREAT PYRENEES

The Great Pyrenees has also been called the "Gentle Giant" of all the predator control dogs. A good Pyrenees knows when to protect and should not provoke a fight. Pyrs have been bred to think for themselves. When guarding livestock, a Pyr will chase a predator off of his territory and then go back to the livestock. If a predator should turn and stand his ground, the Pyr will fight to the death to protect his charges, if necessary. Pyrenees are light on their feet; capable of covering a lot of ground very fast when it is necessary to chase a predator.

Pyrs are far from being stupid, but they can be stubborn. When it comes to obedience training, you need to have a lot of patience. Remember that Pyrs were selectively bred on the basis of their ability to make wise decisions for the benefit of their flocks, not on how quickly they responded to commands.

A stranger would not want to approach the property where a Pyr was on duty if the owner were not present. If the owner is present and gives the okay, the Pyr should be friendly or, at the very least, tolerant of the stranger.

It is not difficult for Pyrs to become couch potatoes if you let them. They enjoy all the comforts of home as much as any human. It is best to teach your Pyr that a specific chair is his, and that he isn't privy to all the furniture in the house. This will relieve you of the constant nudging he will do to be petted if he is sharing the sofa with you while you're watching TV or talking on the phone.

Once a Pyr realizes that guests are welcomed, he is not beyond pestering them for pats and scratches. Being able to send him to his own spot means that you can both relax peacefully and comfortably.

Inside the home, a Pyr will usually choose to sleep on the floor at the foot of your, or your child's, bed (*in* the bed is even better if he can arrange it!) or in the doorway to the bedroom. Outside, a Pyr will sleep by the gate, a doorway, or in a part of the yard where he can see everything around him. A Pyr will do this so that anything or anyone passing would have to go by him first.

Protective and intelligent, the Great Pyrenees is naturally devoted to his family and will go to great lengths to keep them safe.

Children and dogs can make great companions provided they are both taught how to respect and care for one another.

Prys will usually check the perimeter of their yards regularly. Indoors, they have been known to make the rounds of the house, checking on the children in their rooms while they are playing or sleeping. Nor is it at all unusual to see a Pry slowly and unobtrusively follow your children around as if they were livestock to be protected.

Although a Great Pyrenees may not respond to obedience lessons as well as a Golden Retriever or perform all the wonders of a show dog, a well-bred and well-socialized Pyr is extremely tolerant, particularly of children. A Pyr will get up and walk away before he would ever snap at or bite a child.

With that said, no dog should be made to tolerate abusive children. Before bringing a new dog into your home, the children need to be told how to take care of the newcomer and how they must behave around the dog, whether a puppy or an adult.

When you are out walking your Pyr puppy, you will find he will attract attention. Perfect strangers will come up and want to pet and ask about the dog. A Pyr will tend to get between you and the stranger. He won't growl or show any signs of aggression, but quietly and calmly get himself in a protective position.

If the stranger were to step forward, a Pyr tends to lean into the person in a subtle, non-aggressive way, keeping himself between the stranger and the person he is protecting.

Unfortunately, there have been reports of very aggressive and very shy Pyrenees provoking fights with other dogs and biting people in fear. These are not true characteristics of this breed and should *never* be tolerated under any circumstances.

Problems of this kind exist in every breed. Difficult behavior does not come from inbreeding as the novice may be inclined to think. Bad temperament comes from bad breeding. Ill-tempered dogs pass that trait to their offspring. Perhaps not every puppy in the litter will be ill-tempered, but even those who do not manifest this behavior carry the gene to pass on to their offspring.

It is extremely critical when considering the purchase of any dog, particularly a Great Pyrenees, that the buyer go only to someone who is familiar with all the dogs in his or her breeding program, and who puts typical temperament at the top of breeding priorities.

BAD HABITS

Every breed has its good and bad sides, and every puppy in a litter has his own specific personality and quirks. While some puppies in the litter will exhibit certain characteristics to a high degree, other pups in the litter may be at the other end of the scale and have their own set of behavioral idiosyncrasies. Some typical Great Pyrenees problems are digging, running off, and barking.

Digging

A Pyr isn't necessarily digging to escape. He's more apt to be digging a bed, called a pit, in which to sleep. Historically, when

Great Pyrs are known to dig holes in the ground, called pits, in which to sleep. This behavior dates back to when they were used to guard livestock.

An unleashed Great Pyrenees may have the tendency to wander off and check out his surrounding territory. For his own safety, keep your dog on a leash when he is outside.

Pyrs have been out with livestock, they dug holes for their beds. They have done this for centuries, so trying to convince your Pyr that this is no longer necessary may take more than a little effort.

The hole a Pyr digs will usually be in a place from which he can see everything that is going on, usually under a cool bush or tree, or in the middle of your flower or vegetable garden.

Just because the breed has an inclination to dig does not mean you should allow your dog to do this anywhere he chooses. If he digs in an area that you do not want a hole, fill the hole with dirt, put some of his fecal matter on top of the hole, and lightly cover it up with dirt. This will usually keep the dog from digging in that same spot. If you don't do this, catching your dog in the act of digging and making it clear that this is not acceptable might do the trick, but he may try to dig somewhere else.

Running Off

Some Pyrs, once they are off leash in an unfenced area, will be on their way down the road. It is said that Pyrs that do this are just checking out the territory and will return in a few hours. That is all well and good in remote areas, but if you live in the city, you are dealing with traffic and situations in which a dog could get injured, killed, or stolen.

Even if you do live in the country, people with livestock do not take kindly to a large, unfamiliar dog hanging around their animals, and may see your Pyr as a threat. Some sections of the country have livestock laws that permit owners to shoot any animal that even *appears* to threaten their livestock.

If you want to be able to let your Pyr off leash, you need to work with him extensively from puppyhood to respond immediately to the come command.

Barking

Great Pyrenees can be inveterate barkers because of an instinctive reaction to warn their people of anything unusual or out of the ordinary. This is especially true at night—the time of predators! If dealt with early on, this reaction can be kept under control. Unfortunately, too many owners don't pay enough attention to puppy barks, so when it eventually annoys the neighborhood and they can't get their adult dogs to stop, they

Occasionally, puppies may tend to show improper behavior such as biting or digging. Correct these behaviors using firm but positive reinforcement.

have a genuine problem on their hands. When neighbors are complaining and Animal Control is issuing citations, the problem is out of your hands. Barking is the reason why many dogs have to be rehomed.

When your dog is barking, say the dog's name in a firm tone and give the command, "Quiet!" You can use "Stop" or whatever word you want, but use the same command every time.

The Pyrenees usually responds to a firm tone. If the barking continues after you give the command, get a pitcher of water. The next time the dog barks, say his name and the command that you choose in a firm tone, and throw the water (not the pitcher) at the dog. After this happens several times, the dog should stop when you give the command to be quiet. Citronella no-bark collars can also be very effective. Persistence will pay off, but this is not a situation when you can correct the dog only some of the time and expect good results.

A Pyr can have one, all, or none of these habits. They are typical

Great Pyrs are bred to guard their families and warn them of any trespassers. This instinct may lead to barking, which can be controlled with basic obedience.

Providing your Great Pyrenees with a large, fenced-in exercise area will keep him physically stimulated and prevent him from running away.

traits of the breed, however. Being aware and knowing how to deal with them will save you a lot of headaches, and will avoid rethinking your decision in selecting a Great Pyrenees.

Remember every breed has its inherited characteristics or traits. It is just a matter of being aware of what they are and dealing with them properly that determines what kind of a relationship you will have with your dog.

When looking for a puppy, adult, or rescue dog, always ask the breeder what the problem characteristics of the breed are. If the answer is that the breed or the dog has none—go elsewhere. They either just want your money or want to get rid of the dog or puppy they have.

SELECTING the Right Great Pyrenees for You

Once the prospective Pyr owner satisfactorily answers all the questions relating to responsible ownership, he or she will undoubtedly want to rush out and purchase a puppy immediately. Do not act in haste. The purchase of any dog is an important step, because the well-cared-for dog will live with you for many years. In the case of a Great Pyrenees, the breed is known to be highly disease-resistant, and many have been known to live well into their teens. You will undoubtedly want the dog you live with for that length of time to be one you will enjoy.

It is extremely important that your Pyr is purchased from a breeder who has earned a reputation over the years for consistently producing dogs that are mentally and physically sound. Not only is a sound and stable temperament of paramount importance in a large breed of this kind, but there are also a number of diseases that can and do exist in the breed that concern responsible breeders. Unfortunately, the buyer must indeed beware, because there are always those who will exploit a breed for financial gain with no thought given to its health, welfare, or the homes in which the dogs will be living.

When visiting a breeder's kennel, make sure that both the dogs and the facilities are clean and well kept.

Responsible breeders care about their puppies' well-beings and do their best to ensure them healthy and long lives. Six-week-old "Serena" won't be ready to go to her new home for another few weeks.

The only way a breeder can earn a reputation for producing quality animals is through a well-thought-out breeding program in which rigid selectivity is imposed. Selective breeding is aimed at maintaining the virtues of a breed and eliminating genetic weaknesses. This process is time-consuming and costly. Responsible Pyr breeders protect their investments by providing the utmost in prenatal care for their brood matrons and maximum care and nutrition for the resulting offspring. Once the puppies arrive, the knowledgeable breeder initiates a well-thought-out socialization process. The concerned breeder not only keeps the puppy, or adult for that matter, until exactly the right home is found, but also by contract demands that the dog be returned to him in the event that the situation does not work out.

Many of these same breeders are also involved in rescue organizations, and their diligence in placing the dogs in the right foster homes is no less thorough. They provide financial assistance in making the dogs suitable for their foster homes—spaying, neutering, inoculations, and deworming.

The relationship with a responsible breeder does not end when the buyer walks out the door with his or her puppy. The association continues on for the dog's life.

You'll find that good breeders do not let their puppies go to new homes on Christmas or other major holidays or be given as gifts without meeting and talking to the prospective new owners. They will *never* push or pressure prospective owners to buy a puppy.

The governing kennel clubs in different countries maintain lists of local breed clubs and breeders that can lead a prospective dog buyer to responsible breeders of quality stock. If you want to find a respected breeder in your area, contact your local kennel club for recommendations.

You should look for cleanliness in both the dogs and the areas in which the dogs are kept. Cleanliness is the first clue that tells you how much the breeder cares about the dogs he or she owns.

It is extremely important that you know the character and quality of a puppy's parents. Good temperament and good health are inherited, and if the puppy's parents are not sound in these respects, there is not much likelihood that they will produce offspring that are. Never buy a Pyr from anyone who has no knowledge of the puppy's parents or what kind of care a puppy has been given from birth to the time you see him.

A Breeder Checklist

You will find that the Great Pyrenees breeders who are most highly respected and most often recommended have the following characteristics in common:

1. They never breed their females on first heat or at every heat.

2. They only breed dogs that are structurally sound and have been certified free of hip dysplasia by the OFA, GDC, or PennHip™.

3. They breed only animals of sound temperament.

4. They have spay/neuter contracts or have the procedures done before placing the puppies.

5. They provide health, temperament, and hip guarantees in writing.

6. They do not place puppies before eight weeks of age.

7. They properly educate perspective owners on all matters relating to the Great Pyrenees.

8. They are always available to help and answer questions for new owners.

9. They belong to Great Pyrenees Club of America and/or regional breed or all-breed clubs.

10. They follow the Code of Ethics of their national club.

A WORD ABOUT RESCUE

Rescue dogs are the Pyrenees or other breeds that people can no longer keep, possibly due to moving, divorce, family problems, or dog behavior problems. Some dogs are found roaming the streets or are in shelters and pounds. People involved in rescue take these dogs, find out as much as they can about their backgrounds, complete evaluations of the dogs, and place them in suitable homes. Rescue dogs can be any age, from young puppies to much older dogs.

All responsible Pyr breeders assist the rescue organizations in some way, such as taking in rescue dogs, whether the dogs are of their breed or not. Others refer potential Pyr owners to the rescue organization or make donations to rescue funds, and some people underwrite ads in the newspapers offering Great Pyrenees information.

If possible, try to see the parents of the puppy that you are considering. Their overall health and temperaments will indicate what your Great Pyrenees will be like as an adult.

HEALTH CONCERNS

There is every possibility that a reputable breeder resides in your area who will not only be able to provide the right Pyr for you, but also will have both parents of the puppy on the premises. This gives you an opportunity to see firsthand what kind of dogs are in the background of the puppy you are considering. Good breeders are always willing to have you see their dogs and to inspect the facility in which the dogs are raised. These breeders will also be able to discuss problems that exist in the breed with you and how they deal with these problems.

Hip Dysplasia

Simply put, hip dysplasia is a failure of the head of the femur to fit snugly into the acetabulum, with resulting degrees of lameness and faulty movement. The inheritance of the defect is polygenic, which means there is no simple answer to the elimination of the problem. Breeders routinely x-ray their breeding stock and breed only from superior animals that have been graded in the categories deemed acceptable for breeding. While it is important that both the sire and dam have been x-rayed and cleared for breeding, it is just as important that their littermates, grandparents, and so on, have been x-rayed and their history known. Family selection is at least as important as individual selection in the case of polygenic diseases. Asking a breeder the hip status on the parents of the litter, and about the incident of hip dysplasia in their line would be an important question to ask any breeder of Great Pyrenees. As a pet owner, it is important for you to know those individual dogs whose hips might not rate above a grade of fair are able to lead a long and normal life.

Osteosarcoma

Cancer of the bone is not uncommon in the Great Pyrenees, and as we now know through human medicine, tendencies toward certain types of cancer are known to be more prevalent in some families than others. Osteosarcoma manifests itself in the Pyr by a persistent lameness of a leg, and a malignant tumor will develop. Another good question to ask a Pyr breeder is if there have been any occurrences of osteosarcoma or any other cancers in his or her line.

Patella Luxation

This condition is also commonly referred to as "slipping stifles." It is an abnormality of the stifle or knee joint resulting in dislocation

Be prepared to answer breeders' questions concerning your lifestyle and living conditions. They want to ensure that their puppies go to stable, loving, and permanent homes.

of the kneecap (patella). Normally the kneecap is located in a groove at the lower end of the thighbone. It is held in position by strong elastic ligaments. If the groove is insufficiently developed, the kneecap will leave its normal position and slip to one side or the other of the track in which it is normally held. The dog may exhibit an intermittent, but persistent, limp or have difficulty straightening out the knee. In some cases the dog may experience pain. Treatment may include surgery.

Thyroid Disease

The thyroid gland is located in the neck and aids in producing a hormone that controls the metabolism in a dog's body. When the gland malfunctions and reduces its output, a condition called hypothyroidism occurs. Some detectable signs of hypothyroidism include poor hair growth, muscle weakness, loss of appetite, and tiredness.

The condition can be improved with replacement therapy consisting of daily doses of thyroid hormone for a period of six weeks. In some cases, lifetime medication is necessary.

This condition may be initially hard to detect because normal, healthy Great Pyrenees have a lower metabolism than many other dogs. They do not require a lot of exercise, and eat almost half the amount of other dogs their size.

Pyr puppies eat a great deal in their first year because they are growing so fast, but there is a marked slow down around one year of age.

ANESTHETIC SENSITIVITY

The Great Pyrenees has a low tolerance for anesthesia and tranquilization. They require less per pound than a small dog. Always ask your vet if he or she is familiar with this situation in the Great Pyrenees, and make sure the information is added to the dog's medical chart, which should be kept on file. Although most veterinarians know there are different levels of sensitivity in this respect, your vet may not be aware of the breed's problem in this area.

QUESTIONS AND ANSWERS

Describing the diseases that can affect the Pyr does not indicate that all Pyr lines are afflicted with them. However, the responsible breeder will always be more than happy to discuss his or her experience, if any, with genetic-related problems.

38

A healthy puppy should be playful, outgoing, and happy. Seven-week-old "Edie" and "Liz" are perfect examples of well-adjusted puppies.

All breeds of dog have genetic problems that must be addressed. Just because a male and female Great Pyrenees do not have health complications does not mean their pedigrees are free of something that might be entirely incapacitating. Again, rely upon recommendations from national kennel clubs or local breed clubs when looking for a breeder.

As we have mentioned previously, do not be surprised if a concerned breeder asks many questions about you and the environment in which your Pyr will be raised. Good breeders are just as concerned with the quality of the homes to which their dogs are going as you are in obtaining a sound and healthy dog.

Do not think a good Pyr puppy can only come from a large kennel. On the contrary, many of today's best breeders raise dogs in their homes as a hobby. It is important, however, that you not allow yourself to fall into the hands of an irresponsible backyard breeder. Backyard breeders separate themselves from the hobby breeder through their disregard for the health of their breeding stock. They do not test their stock for genetic problems, nor are they concerned with how or where their puppies are raised. We offer one important bit of advice to the prospective Pyr buyer. If the person is attempting to sell you a puppy with no questions asked–*go elsewhere!*

RECOGNIZING A HEALTHY PUPPY

Pyr breeders never release their puppies until the puppies have been given their puppy shots. Normally, this is at about eight to ten weeks of age. After this age, they will bond extremely well with their new owners, and the puppies are entirely weaned. Nursing puppies receive temporary immunization from their mother. Once weaned, however, a puppy is highly susceptible to many infectious diseases that can be transmitted via the hands and clothing of people. Therefore, make sure your puppy is fully inoculated before he leaves his home environment, and know when any additional inoculations should be given.

Above all, the Pyr puppy you buy should be happy, outgoing, and self-confident. The Pyr's protective instinct develops in adulthood. A shy or suspicious puppy is definitely a poor choice, as is one that appears sick and listless. Selecting a puppy because you feel sorry for him will undoubtedly lead to heartache and difficulty, to say nothing of the veterinary costs that you may incur in restoring the puppy's health.

Ask the breeder if it is possible to take the puppy you are interested in away from his littermates into another room or another part of the kennel. The smells will remain the same for the puppy, so he should still feel secure and maintain his outgoing personality, but it will give you an opportunity to inspect the puppy more closely.

A healthy little Pyr puppy will be strong and sturdy to the touch, never bony or obese and bloated. The inside of the puppy's ears should be pink and clean. Dark discharge or a bad odor could indicate ear mites, which is a sure sign of poor maintenance. The healthy Pyr puppy's breath smells sweet, the unique smell that dog breeders lovingly call "puppy breath." The teeth are clean and white, and there should never be any malformation of the mouth or jaw. The puppy's eyes should be clear, bright, and have a soft, almost wise look typical of a Pyr baby. Eyes that appear runny and irritated indicate serious problems.

Whether male or female, Great Pyrenees are capable of becoming wonderful, lifelong companions. However, do consider that a male Pyr can be 15 to 20 pounds heavier than a female.

There should be no sign of discharge from the nose, nor should it be crusted or runny. Coughing and diarrhea are danger signals as are any eruptions on the skin. The coat should be soft and lustrous.

The healthy Pyr puppy's front legs should be straight as posts, strong and true. Even these giant breed puppies will appear active, agile, and strong, although they may stumble over their own feet occasionally. Do not mistake this for unsoundness. If you have any doubts, discuss them with the breeder.

MALE OR FEMALE?

While both the male and the female Great Pyrenees are capable of becoming excellent companions, consider the fact that a male Pyr will be larger, sometimes 15 to 20 pounds heavier than a female, and he will have all the muscle power to go with the extra weight. Give serious consideration to your own strength and stature.

There are other sex-related differences to consider as well. While the Great Pyrenees is a clean breed and easy to housetrain, some males can provide a problem. The male of any breed has a natural instinct to lift his leg and "mark" his territory. Thankfully one of the virtues of the Great Pyrenees is, unlike a macho Chihuahua or terrier, the male Pyr is much less likely to "mark" the inside of your home. Females, on the other hand, have their own set of problems. Females have their semi-annual heat cycles that commence at about six months of age. During these heat cycles of approximately 21 days, the female must be confined to avoid soiling her surroundings with the bloody discharge that accompanies estrus. Like everything else about the Great Pyrenees, the bloody discharge is a lot in comparison to smaller breeds where the discharge is usually referred to as "spotting." There are britches sold at pet shops that assist in keeping the female in heat from soiling the area in which she lives. She must also be carefully watched to prevent males from gaining access to her or she will become pregnant. *Do not expect the "marauding male" to be deterred by the britches if your female has them on!*

Both of these sexually related problems can be avoided by having your pet Pyr spayed or neutered. Spaying the female and neutering the male saves the pet owner all the headaches of sexually related problems without changing the character of his Pyr. If there is any change at all in the altered Pyr, it is in making the dog an even more amiable companion. Above all, altering your pet helps decrease the serious pet overpopulation problems that exist worldwide.

SELECTING A SHOW-PROSPECT PUPPY

If you are considering a show career for your puppy, all the foregoing regarding soundness and health apply here as well. It must be remembered though, spaying and castration are not reversible procedures and, once done, eliminate the possibility of ever breeding or showing your Pyr in conformation shows. Altered dogs can, however, be shown in obedience trials and many other competitive events.

There are a good number of additional points to be considered for the show dog as well. First of all, it should be remembered that the most any breeder could offer is an opinion on the show potential of a particular puppy. The most promising eight-week-old Pyr puppy can grow up to be an average adult. A breeder has no control over this. It is sometimes said that an unknowing new owner can ruin a show-prospect puppy in about three weeks with improper feeding and exercise, and this certainly holds true with a giant breed puppy like the Pyr.

Any predictions breeders make about a puppy's future are based on their experiences with past litters that have produced winning show dogs. It is obvious the more successful a breeder has been in producing winning Pyrs over the years, the broader his or her base of comparison will be.

A puppy's potential as a show dog is determined by how closely he adheres to the breed standard. While most breeders concur there is no such thing as a sure thing when it comes to predicting winners, they are also quick to agree that the older a puppy is, the better your chances are of making any predictions.

It makes little difference to the pet owner if his Pyr is a little high in the rear or doesn't have all the exact curves and angles the standard calls for. These faults do not interfere with a Pyr becoming a healthy, loving companion. However, these flaws would keep that Pyr from a top-winning show career.

While it certainly behooves the prospective buyer of a show puppy to be as familiar with the standard of the breed as possible, it is even more important for the buyer to contact a successful and respected breeder of winning Pyrs. The experienced breeder

Before entering your Great Pyrenees in conformation shows, make sure that he adheres to the breed standard.

knows there are certain age-related shortcomings in a young Pyr that maturity will take care of, and there are other faults that completely eliminate the puppy from consideration as a show prospect.

Breeders are always looking for the right homes in which to place their show-prospect puppies. They can be particularly helpful when they know you plan to show one of their dogs.

The important thing to remember in choosing your first show-prospect puppy is that cuteness may not be consistent with quality. While showmanship and a charismatic personality are critical to a show dog's success in the ring, those qualities are the frosting on the cake, so to speak. They are the characteristics that put the well-made Pyr over the top.

An extroverted or particularly loving puppy in the litter might decide he belongs to you. If you are simply looking for a pet, that is the puppy for you. However, if you are genuinely interested in showing your Pyr, you must keep your head and, without disregarding good temperament, give serious consideration to what the standard says a show type Great Pyrenees must be.

Although good looks and a charismatic personality are part of a dog's success in the show ring, they are not everything. Consult the breed standard for an example of an ideal Great Pyrenees.

PUPPY OR ADULT?

A young puppy is not your only option when contemplating the purchase of a Pyr. In some cases, an adult dog may be just the answer. It certainly eliminates the trials and tribulations of house-training, chewing, and the myriad of other problems associated with a young puppy.

Sometimes adult Pyrs are available from homes or kennels that breed show dogs. Retired from the ring or no longer being used for breeding, the older dog would be far happier in a family situation where he can watch TV, take hikes, and be a part of a family instead of living out his life in a kennel run.

Fully mature Pyrs can also be available through rescue organizations. These dogs, thoroughly evaluated by the respective organization, can prove to be wonderful companions once they are rehomed.

Adult Pyrs can adjust to their new homes with relative ease. Most new owners are amazed at how quickly these adult dogs become devoted to their new families! After all, a Pyr lives to protect and love his family. Even those

Although Pyr puppies are adorable and often hard to resist, they may not be the best choice for some people. Carefully consider whether a puppy or an adult Great Pyrenees is right for your lifestyle.

raised in a kennel seem to blossom in a family environment.

An adult Pyr that has been given kind and loving care in his previous home could be the perfect answer for the elderly or someone who is forced to be away from home during the day. While it would be unreasonable to expect a young puppy not to relieve himself in the house if you are gone for more than just a few hours, it would be surprising to find a housetrained Pyr who, in adulthood, would willingly even *consider* relieving himself in his home.

A few adult Pyrs may become set in their ways and, while you may not have to contend with the problems of puppyhood, realize there is the rare Pyr adult that might have developed habits that do not entirely suit you or your lifestyle. Arrange to bring an adult Pyr into your home on a trial basis so you will not be obligated if you decide you are incompatible.

IMPORTANT PAPERS

The purchase of any purebred dog entitles you to some very important documents: a health record containing an inoculation list, a copy of the dog's pedigree, the registration certificate, a diet sheet, and a sales contract.

Health Record

Most Pyr puppies have been inoculated by the time they are seven or eight weeks old. These inoculations temporarily protect the puppies against distemper, hepatitis, leptospirosis, and canine parvovirus. Depending on where the breeder is located, puppies may also be vaccinated against coronavirus and Lyme disease. In most cases, rabies inoculations are not given until a puppy is four months of age or older.

There is a series of inoculations developed to combat these infectious diseases, and it is extremely important that you obtain a record of the shots your puppy has been given and the dates upon which they were administered. The veterinarian you choose will be able to continue on with the appropriate inoculation series as needed.

Pedigree

The pedigree is your dog's family tree. The breeder must supply you with a copy of this document authenticating your puppy's ancestors back to at least the third generation. All purebred dogs have a pedigree. The pedigree does not imply that a dog is of show quality. It is simply a chronological list of ancestors.

Registration Certificate

The registration certificate is the canine's birth certificate, issued by a country's governing kennel club. When you transfer the ownership of your Pyr from the breeder's name to yours, the transaction is entered on this certificate, and once mailed to the kennel club, it is permanently recorded in their computerized files. Keep all these documents in a safe place because you will need them when you visit your veterinarian or if you ever wish to breed or show your Pyr.

Diet Sheet

Your Pyr is happy and healthy because the breeder has been carefully feeding and caring for him. Most breeders give the new

Don't be surprised if a breeder asks you as many questions as you ask her—by answering her questions honestly, she can help you to select the puppy that suits you best.

Your breeder should supply you with a diet sheet. Maintain this original diet and make any changes gradually to avoid stomach upset.

owner a written record that details the amount and kind of food a puppy has been receiving. Follow these recommendations to the letter at least for the first month or two after the puppy comes to live with you.

The diet sheet should indicate the number of times a day your puppy has been fed and the kind of vitamin supplementation, if any, he has been receiving. Following the prescribed procedure will reduce the chance of upset stomach and loose stools.

Usually a breeder's diet sheet projects the increases and changes in food that will be necessary as your puppy grows from week to week. If the sheet does not include this information, ask the breeder for suggestions regarding increases and the eventual changeover to adult food.

In the unlikely event that you are not supplied with a diet sheet by the breeder and are unable to get one, your veterinarian will be able to advise you in this respect. There are countless foods now being manufactured that meet the nutritional needs of puppies and growing dogs. A trip down the pet aisle at your supermarket or pet supply store will prove just how many choices you have. Two important tips to remember: Read labels carefully for content; and when dealing with established, reliable manufacturers, you are more likely to get what you pay for.

Sales Contract

The reputable Great Pyrenees breeder will supply a written agreement that lists everything that he or she is responsible for in connection with the sale of the dog. The contract will also list all the things the buyer is responsible for before the sale is actually final. The contract should be dated and signed by both the seller and the buyer. Sales contracts vary, but all assurances and anything that is an exception to the outright and final sale should be itemized. Some of these conditions are as follows:

• Sale is contingent upon dog passing a veterinarian's examination within two to three days after he leaves the seller's premises. Clear statement of refund policy.

• Any conditions regarding seller's requirement for neutering or spaying of dog sold.

• Indication that a "limited registration"accompanies the dog (that is, the dog is ineligible to have offspring registered by the AKC).

• Arrangements that must be followed in the event the buyer is unable to keep the dog regardless of length of time that elapses after sale.

• Conditions that exist if the dog develops genetic hip, eye, heart, temperament, or any other relevant genetic disorders at maturity.

TEMPERAMENT AND SOCIALIZATION

Temperament is both inherited and learned. Poor treatment and lack of proper socialization can ruin a dog's inherited good temperament. A Pyr puppy that has inherited bad temperament is a poor risk as a show dog and should certainly never be bred. In fact, a Great Pyrenees with poor temperament is a dangerous weapon and not a suitable pet. Therefore, it is critical that you obtain a happy puppy from a breeder who is determined to produce good temperaments and has taken all the necessary steps to provide early socialization.

Temperaments in the same litter can range from strong-willed and outgoing on the high end of the scale to reserved and retiring at the low end. A puppy that is so bold and strong-willed as to be foolhardy and uncontrollable could easily be a difficult adult that needs a very firm hand. In a breed as large and strong as the Pyr, this would hardly be a dog for the mild-mannered and reserved or physically frail owner. In every human/canine relationship, there must be a pack leader and a follower. In order to achieve his full potential, the Pyr must have an owner who remains in charge at all times. The Pyr wants and needs this kind of relationship.

It is important to remember that a Pyr puppy may be as happy as a clam living at home with you and your family, but if the

All puppies, even those from the same litter, have their own unique personalities. Obtaining a Great Pyrenees puppy from a reputable breeder will help ensure sound health and temperament.

socialization begun by the breeder is not continued, that sunny disposition will not extend outside your front door. From the day the young Pyr arrives at your home, you must be committed to accompanying him on an unending pilgrimage to meet and co-exist with all human beings and animals. Do not worry about the Pyr's protective instinct. This comes with maturity. *Never* encourage aggressive behavior in your puppy, nor should there be any reason for him to fear strangers.

Your puppy should go everywhere with you—the post office, the market, the shopping mall—wherever. Be prepared to create a stir wherever you go. The public seems to hold a special admiration for the Pyr. While they might not want to approach a mature dog, most people are quite taken with the Pyr puppy and will undoubtedly want to pet your youngster. There is nothing in the world better for the puppy!

If your puppy backs away from a stranger, give the person a treat to offer him. You must *insist* that your young Pyr be amenable to the attention of any strangers you approve of, regardless of sex, age, or race. It is not up to your puppy to decide whom he will or will not tolerate. You are in charge; you must call the shots.

If your Pyr has a show career in his future, there are other things in addition to just being handled that will have to be taught. All show dogs must learn to have their mouths opened and their teeth inspected by the judge. Males must be accustomed to having their testicles touched, because the judge must determine that male dogs are intact. These inspections must begin in puppyhood and be done on a regular basis.

All Pyrs must learn to get along with other dogs as well as with humans. If you are fortunate enough to have a "puppy preschool" or dog training class nearby, attend as regularly as you possibly can. A young Pyr that has been exposed to other dogs from

In order to become well-adjusted adult dogs, puppies need the proper socialization at an early age. A puppy that has been exposed to other dogs from puppyhood will accept them more readily.

There are many factors that contribute to a pet's happiness and well-being, such as a healthy living environment, good care, and unconditional love.

puppyhood will learn to adapt and accept other dogs much more readily than one that seldom sees strange dogs.

THE ADOLESCENT GREAT PYRENEES

You will find it amazing how quickly the youngster you brought home begins to develop into a full-grown Great Pyrenees. Some lines shoot up to full size very rapidly, while others mature more slowly. At about six or seven months of age, most Pyr puppies become lanky and ungainly, growing in and out of proportion seemingly from one day to the next, which is not surprising because the average Great Pyrenees puppy weighs between 60 and 70 pounds during this time!

Somewhere between 12 to 18 months of age, your Pyr will have attained his full height. However, body and muscle development continues until three years of age in some lines and up to four or more in others.

Food needs increase during this growth period, and the average Pyr seems as if he can never get enough to eat. On occasion, however, there's the rare Pyr that experiences a very finicky stage in his eating habits and seems to eat enough only to keep from starving. Think of Pyr puppies as individualistic as children and act accordingly.

The amount of food you give your Pyr should be adjusted to how much he will readily consume at each meal. If the entire meal is eaten quickly, add a small amount to the next feeding and continue to do so as the need increases. This method will ensure that you are giving your puppy enough food, but you must also pay close attention to the dog's appearance and condition, because you do not want a puppy to become overweight or obese.

At eight weeks of age, a Pyr puppy is eating three to four meals a day. By the time your pup is three months old, he can do well on two meals a day with perhaps a snack in the middle of the day. If your puppy does not eat the food offered, he is either not hungry or not well. Your dog will eat when he is hungry. If you suspect the dog is not well, take him to the veterinarian.

The adolescent period is a particularly important one, because your Pyr must learn all the household and social rules he will live by for the rest of his life. Your patience and commitment during this time will not only produce an obedient canine good citizen, but will forge a bond between you that will grow and ripen into a wonderful relationship.

STANDARD for the Great Pyrenees

A s far back in time as the Great Pyrenees can be traced, the same characteristics have always been valued in the breed. The dog had to be large enough and strong enough to handle predators of all sizes and degrees of aggressiveness. He had to be protective and calm in order to coexist with the flocks he attended. These characteristics typify the breed and remain paramount in the minds of today's Great Pyrenees breeders.

Attempts to classify and name the important characteristics of a breed—both mental and physical—were the forerunners of what are known today as the breed standards. Knowledgeable individuals in the breed wrote the original standards for their peers. The descriptions were used primarily as checklists or blueprints to breed by and served as reminders so important points of conformation would not be lost.

Today's Great Pyrenees breed standard describes a dog that is entirely capable of performing the duties he has been called upon to perform for thousands of years. It includes a description of ideal structure, temperament, coat, color, and the manner in which the breed moves. All of these descriptions relate directly to the breed's original purpose.

As stated, breed standards are used by breeders to assist them in breeding for a goal of perfection. While no dog is absolutely perfect, the dogs that adhere closest to the ideal are what breeders will determine are show or breeding stock. Dogs that deviate to any great extent are considered companion or pet stock.

Dog show judges to compare actual dogs to the ideal also use the standard. The dog adhering closest to this ideal is then the winner of the class and so on down the line.

OFFICIAL STANDARD FOR THE GREAT PYRENEES

General Appearance—The Great Pyrenees dog conveys the distinct impression of elegance and unsurpassed beauty combined with great overall size and majesty. He has a white or principally white coat that may contain markings of badger, gray, or varying shades of tan. He possesses a keen intelligence and a kindly, while regal, expression. Exhibiting a unique elegance of bearing and movement, his soundness and coordination show unmistakably

According to the standard, the Great Pyrenees has an elegant beauty, complete with a lustrous coat and impressive size.

the purpose for which he has been bred, the strenuous work of guarding the flocks in all kinds of weather on the steep mountain slopes of the Pyrenees.

Size, Proportion, Substance—*Size*—The height at the withers ranges from 27 inches to 32 inches for dogs and from 25 inches to 29 inches for bitches. A 27 inch dog weighs about 100 pounds and a 25 inch bitch weighs about 85 pounds. Weight is in proportion to the overall size and structure. *Proportion*—The Great Pyrenees is a balanced dog with the height measured at the withers being somewhat less than the length of the body measured from the point of the shoulder to the rearmost projection of the upper thigh (buttocks). These proportions create a somewhat rectangular dog, slightly longer than it is tall. Front and rear angulation are balanced. *Substance*—The Great Pyrenees is a dog of medium substance whose coat deceives those wh do not feel the bone and muscle. Commensurate with his size and impression of elegance there is sufficient bone and muscle to provide a

The Great Pyrenees' strength, size, and protective instinct make him a valued and respected breed.

balance with the frame. *Faults*—Size—Dogs and bitches under minimum size or over maximum size. *Substance*—Dogs too heavily boned or too lightly boned to be in balance with their frame.

Head—Correct head and expression are essential to the breed. The head is not heavy in proportion to the size of the dog. It is wedge shaped with a slightly rounded crown. *Expression*—The expression is elegant, intelligent and contemplative. *Eyes*—Medium sized, almond shaped, set slightly obliquely, rich dark brown. Eyelids are close fitting with black rims. *Ears*—Small to medium in size, V-shaped with rounded tips, set on at eye level, normally carried low, flat, and close to the head. There is a characteristic meeting of the hair of the upper and lower face which forms a line from the outer corner of the eye to the base of the ear. *Skull and Muzzle*—The muzzle is approximately equal in length to the back skull. The width and length of the skull are approximately equal. The muzzle blends smoothly with the skull. The cheeks are flat. There is sufficient fill under the eyes. A slight

The Great Pyrenees should convey an intelligent and contemplative expression.

furrow exists between the eyes. There is no apparent stop. The boney eyebrow ridges are slightly developed. Lips are tight fitting with the upper lip just covering the lower lip. There is a strong lower jaw. The nose and lips are black. *Teeth*—A scissor bite is preferred, but a level bite is acceptable. It is not unusual to see dropped (receding) lower central incisor teeth. *Faults*— Too heavy head (St. Bernard or Newfoundland-like). Too narrow or small skull. Foxy appearance. Presence of an apparent stop. Missing pigmentation on nose, eye rims, or lips. Eyelids round, triangular, loose

As Ch. Snowbear Ramona Lisa models, the Great Pyr's neck should be strongly muscled and of medium length.

or small. Overshot, undershot, wry mouth.

Neck, Topline, Body—*Neck*—Strongly muscled and of medium length, with minimal dewlap. *Topline*—The backline is level. *Body*—The chest is moderately broad. The rib cage is well sprung, oval in shape, and of sufficient depth to reach the elbows. Back and loin are broad and strongly coupled with some tuck-up. The croup is gently sloping with the tail set on just below the level of the back. *Tail*—The tailbones are of sufficient length to reach the hock. The tail is well plumed, carried low in repose and may be carried over the back, "making the wheel," wheel aroused. When present, a "shepherd's crook" at the end of the tail accentuates the plume. When gaiting, the tail may be carried either over the back or low. Both carriages are equally correct. *Fault*—Barrel ribs.

Forequarters—*Shoulders*—The shoulders are well laid back, well muscled, and lie close to the body. The upper arm meets the shoulder blade at approximately a right angle. The upper arm angles backward from the point of the shoulder to the elbow and is never perpendicular to the ground. The length of the shoulder blade and the upper arm is approximately equal. The height from the ground to the elbow appears approximately equal to the height from the elbow to the withers. *Forelegs*—The legs are of sufficient bone and muscle to provide a balance with the frame. The elbows are close to the body and point directly to the rear when standing and gaiting. The forelegs, when viewed from the side, are located directly under the withers and are straight and vertical to the ground. The elbows, when viewed from the front, are set in a straight line from the point of the shoulder to the wrist. Front pasterns are strong and flexible. Each foreleg carries a single dewclaw. *Front Feet*—Rounded, close-cupped, well padded, toes well arched.

Hindquarters—The angulation of the hindquarters is similar in degree to that of the forequarters. *Thighs*—Strongly muscular upper thighs extend from the pelvis at right angles. The upper thigh is the same length as the lower thigh, creating moderate stifle joint angulation when viewed in profile. The rear pastern (metatarsus) is of medium length and perpendicular to the ground

The Great Pyrenees' coat should be all white or white with markings of gray, badger, reddish brown, or varying shades of tan.

as the dog stands naturally. This produces a moderate degree of angulation in the hock joint, when viewed from the side. The hindquarters from hip to the rear pastern are straight and parallel, as viewed from the rear. The rear legs are of sufficient bone and muscle to provide a balance with the frame. Double dewclaws are located on each rear leg. *Rear Feet*—The rear feet have a structural tendency to toe out slightly. This breed characteristic is not to be confused with cow-hocks. The rear feet, like the forefeet, are rounded, close-cupped, well padded with toes well arched. *Fault*—Absence of double dewclaws on each rear leg.

Coat—The weather resistant double coat consists of a long, flat, thick, outer coat of coarse hair, straight or slightly undulating, and lying over a dense, fine, woolly undercoat. The coat is more profuse about the neck and shoulders where it forms a ruff or mane which is more pronounced in males. Longer hair on the tail forms a plume. There is feathering along the back of the front legs and along the back of the thighs, giving a "pantaloon" effect. The hair on the face and ears is shorter and of finer texture. Correctness of coat is more important than abundance of coat. *Faults*—Curly coat. Stand-off coat (Samoyed type).

Color—White or white markings of gray, badger, reddish brown, or varying shades of tan. Markings of varying size may appear on the ears, head (including a full face mask), tail, and as

Despite his large size, the Great Pyrenees moves with ease, exhibiting both power and agility.

The true temperament of a Great Pyrenees is loyal, confident, gentle, and affectionate, especially with his human playmates.

a few body spots. The undercoat may be white or shaded. All of the above described colorings and locations are characteristic of the breed and equally correct. **Fault**—Outer coat markings covering more than one third of the body.

Gait—The Great Pyrenees moves smoothly and elegantly, true and straight ahead, exhibiting both power and agility. The stride is well balanced with good reach and strong drive. The legs tend to move toward the center line as speed increases. Ease and efficiency of movement are more important than speed.

Temperament—Character and temperament are of utmost importance. In nature, the Great Pyrenees is confident, gentle, and affectionate. While territorial and protective of his flock or family when necessary, his general demeanor is one of quiet composure, both patient and tolerant. He is strong willed, independent and somewhat reserved, yet attentive, fearless and loyal to his charges both human and animal.

Although the Great Pyrenees may appear reserved in the show ring, any sign of excessive shyness, nervousness, or aggression to humans is unacceptable and must be considered an extremely serious fault.

Approved June 12, 1990
Effective August 1, 1990

CARING for Your Great Pyrenees

FEEDING AND NUTRITION

Following the diet sheet provided by the breeder from whom you obtained your puppy is the best way to make sure your Pyr is obtaining the right amount and correct type of food for his age. Do your best not to change the puppy's diet in order to avoid digestive problems and diarrhea. Diarrhea is very serious in young puppies because they can dehydrate very rapidly, causing severe problems or even death.

If it is necessary to change your puppy's diet for any reason, it should never be done abruptly. Begin by adding a quarter cup of the new food and reduce the old product by the same amount. Gradually increase the amount of the new food over a week or ten days until the meal consists entirely of the new product. A puppy's digestive system is extremely delicate. *Any* changes you make in what he eats should be done carefully and slowly.

The amount of food you give your Pyr puppy should also be adjusted carefully. Give the puppy his entire meal, wait 10 or 15

A puppy's stomach can be quite sensitive. If you have to adjust the puppy's original diet, do so gradually to avoid digestive problems.

minutes, and then remove dish. If the puppy consumes the entire meal, add a small amount to his next meal. There is the occasional Pyr puppy that is a true glutton and will eat more than he needs to stay healthy. As a rule of thumb, you should be able to feel the ribs and backbone with just a slight layer of fat and muscle over them. The puppy should be firm to the touch, not sloppy with rolls of loose flesh.

It is especially important that your puppy doesn't gain an excessive amount of weight during his first year. Excess weight exacts a heavy toll on the slowly developing skeletal structure of a Great Pyrenees. The Pyr's framework is extremely vulnerable during this early period of life, and you must avoid any undue stress being placed on it. Do not even allow your young Pyr to jump down from heights like a bed, sofa, or the back of a truck or van.

Although it is not as prevalent in Great Pyrenees as it is in many of the large and giant breeds, considering what we now know about bloat and torsion, avoiding large meals is recommended. It is better to feed smaller meals two or even three times daily, instead of one large meal.

As a result of the Pyr's low metabolism and even lower exercise needs, the adult dog will normally eat about half the amount consumed by other dogs his size. A puppy eats a great deal because he is growing so rapidly. However, this slows down around a year of age, and the average adult Pyr will eat about four to five cups of food a day. In the summer months when it is hot, the Pyr is not as active and will eat about two to three cups of food a day.

Some owners feel that a reduced appetite needs to be stimulated, and will try to coax their dogs into eating more by buying different and special foods or by cooking exotic meals for them. All of this is entirely unnecessary as long as your dog is healthy and not undernourished.

Balanced Diets

In the US, dog foods must meet standards set by the Subcommittee on Canine Nutrition of the National Research Council in order to qualify as complete and balanced. As proof of compliance, dog food manufacturers list the ingredients of their product on every box, bag, or can. The ingredients are listed by weight in descending order.

63

It is very important that you closely monitor your Pyr's weight during his first year of life. Excess weight can be detrimental to the Great Pyr's slowly developing skeletal structure.

The Great Pyrenees does not need a high-fat or high-protein diet because this is not a high-energy breed. Keep the protein content of a Pyr's diet down to a level of 26 percent or below. Fat content should not exceed a total of 14 to 18 percent. Fat is the last thing you want your Pyr to be!

Do not feed your Pyr sugar products or products that contain sugar to any high degree. Excessive amounts of sugars can lead to severe dental problems and unwanted weight gain.

To achieve optimum health and condition, make sure that your Pyr has a constant supply of fresh, clean water and a balanced diet containing the essential nutrients in correct proportions. This can be achieved with a good quality kibble plus a small amount of canned, fresh, or cooked meat. Pet stores and supermarkets carry a wide selection of dog foods manufactured by respected firms. An important thing to remember in selecting these foods is that all dogs are meat-eating animals. Animal protein and fats are absolutely essential to the well-being of any breed of dog.

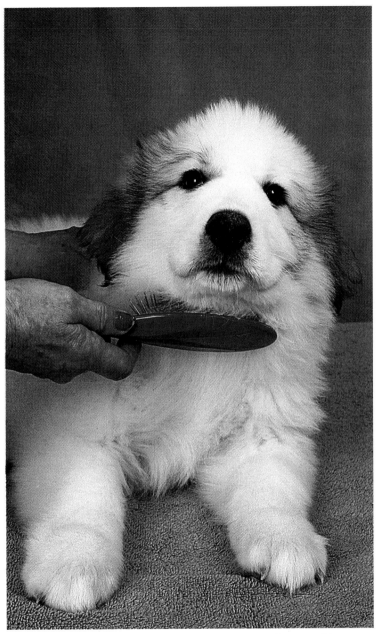

Regularly brushing your Pyr's coat will keep it clean and lustrous and keep shedding to a minimum.

Oversupplementation

A great deal of controversy exists today regarding the orthopedic problems that exist in all dogs such as hip, elbow, and patella (knee) dysplasia. Long-standing, popular opinion has always dictated that these problems, and a wide variety of chronic skin conditions, are entirely hereditary. However, there is growing contingency that overuse of mineral and vitamin supplements in puppies and young dogs can exacerbate, if not cause, these ailments.

When vitamins are used, the prescribed amount should never be exceeded. Some breeders insist all recommended dosages be cut in half when used with today's heavily fortified commercial foods.

Dogs do not care if food looks like a hot dog or a wedge of cheese. They only care about the food's smell and taste. Products manufactured to look like other foods are designed to appeal to the humans who buy them. These foods often contain high amounts of preservatives, sugars, and dyes, none of which are suitable for your dog.

Special Diets

There are a number of commercially prepared diets for dogs with special dietary needs. The overweight, underweight, or geriatric dog can have his nutritional needs met, as can puppies and growing dogs. The calorie content of these foods is adjusted accordingly.

Common sense must prevail. What works for humans works for dogs as well. Too many calories and too little exercise will increase weight; stepping up exercise and reducing the calorie count will bring weight down.

GROOMING AND BATHING

Although Pyrs do not require any clipping or trimming, they do need regular brushing to keep their coats clean, odor-free, and healthy. Brushing also decreases the amount of shedding.

You will need to invest in a slicker brush that has short, angled bristles and a steel comb to remove any debris that collects in the longer furnishings. A comb that has fine and coarse teeth is ideal. You will be using this equipment for many years so buy the best items that you can afford.

Pyr puppies have soft, cottony coats that seem to attract dirt. A Pyr puppy's coat begins to change into an adult coat when he is

Regular grooming sessions combined with an all-over body check will help you to stay on top of your dog's physical condition.

around three to four months of age, but the change is not complete until the dog is somewhere between 10 and 14 months of age.

If a Pyr has been spayed or neutered, the coat can sometimes grow longer and/or thicker with more undercoat, which may require additional brushing and care. Owners who have spayed or neutered older Pyrs that are working livestock or live in areas where the undergrowth has stickers and thorns usually trim the hair on the back of the front legs, the rear legs, hocks, and the underside of the chest and stomach, which makes the coat easier to maintain.

Shaving a Pyr's coat does not cool him off in hot weather. In fact, it is dangerous because the dog becomes susceptible to sunburn and heatstroke. The Pyr's double coat not only keeps him warm in cold weather, but also insulates and cools him off in hot weather. Pyrs normally shed most of their undercoats around the beginning of summer when it is hot. This is enough to keep them cool. It is amazing how cleaver Mother Nature can be!

Regularly grooming your dog also gives you the opportunity to keep on top of his physical condition. If your dog is licking himself and causing an irritation, try applying a product called Bitter Apple™, a foul-tasting, non-toxic liquid. You can also trim his nails, clean his ears, and check his teeth during grooming sessions.

The Pyr has a double coat—a soft undercoat and a coarser outer coat. This helps the coat to shed and not mat as much as a Samoyed's or Chow Chow's coat would. Although you only need to brush your Pyr once a week, daily brushing is permitted. Most Pyrs will not object to a daily brushing.

Part the hair and brush the coat from the skin out to prevent mats. While the coat is shedding, you will want to brush daily if possible. This helps release the dead coat and makes it easier for the new coat to come in. Mats are inclined to occur around the neck, behind the ears, under the tail, and on the rear legs.

Some Pyrs do not like their rear legs or tails brushed. They will pull away to avoid letting you brush these areas. They are simply trying to get their way, and it is up to you to make it clear that your way is the way it will be done.

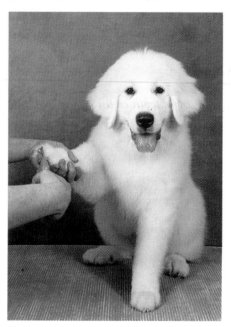

Trimming your dog's nails is an important part of his grooming routine. Also check for cracked footpads and tender or swollen areas.

NAILS

A good time to accustom your Pyr to having his nails trimmed and his feet inspected is during his grooming sessions. Always inspect your dog's feet for cracked pads and check between the toes for splinters and thorns, paying particular attention to any swollen or tender areas.

We suggest attending to your dog's nails at least every six to eight weeks. Long nails on a Pyr are not only unattractive, but

Proper oral hygiene keeps your Pyr's teeth clean and his breath fresh.

they weaken the foot. The nails of a Pyr that isn't exercising outdoors on rough terrain will grow long very quickly. Do not allow the nails to become overgrown and then xpect to cut them back easily. Each nail has a blood vessel running through the center called the quick, which grows close to the end of the nail and contains very sensitive nerve endings. If the nail is allowed to grow too long, it will be impossible to cut it back to a proper length without cutting into the quick, which causes the dog severe pain. It can also result in a great deal of bleeding that can be very difficult to stop.

Nails can be trimmed with canine nail clippers or an electric nail grinder (also called a drummel). Use the fine grinding disc, allowing you to trim back the nail a little bit at a time, which decreases the chance of blood flow. You can easily see the quick on white nails, but dark nails make it practically impossible to see where the quick ends. Regardless of which nail-trimming device

Exercise gives your Great Pyrenees the opportunity to release excess energy or stress and maintain a good physical condition.

is used, you must proceed with caution and remove only a small portion of the nail at a time.

If the quick is nipped in the trimming process, there are a number of blood-clotting products available at pet shops that will almost immediately stem the flow of blood. It is wise to have one of these products on hand in case your dog breaks a nail.

Pyrs have dewclaws (extra toes) on both their front and rear feet. The rear legs have double dewclaws. These nails also need to be trimmed regularly, so that they do not curl around into the pad.

Regular brushing practically eliminates the need for giving your Pyr a wet bath. If your dog finds his way into some foul-smelling substance, there are many dry bath products that can be used to clean the coat and eliminate odor.

Care should always be given to your dog's oral hygiene. If your dog has been accustomed to chewing hard dog biscuits, large rawhide bones, or any of the wide variety of Nylabone™ products since puppyhood, it is unlikely that he will have any dental problems. This chewing activity greatly assists in removing dental plaque, which is the major cause of tooth decay. Any sign of redness of the gums or tooth decay merits expert attention.

Although good temperament is inherited, you can help your Great Pyrenees to become a well-adjusted and happy dog by providing him with the opportunity to meet many different people.

EXERCISE

The Pyr that is given opportunity to exercise on his own or with you is a much happier and healthier dog than one that is not. Any dog that expends his energy in physical activity is far less apt to become mischievous and destructive in the home. Although puppies should never be forced to exercise, they should be encouraged to do so. Your young Pyr can enjoy a walk on lead, a romp through the park, or a jog at the beach. However, until the dog is mature, and only then if you have properly conditioned him, can he be exposed to more arduous and lengthy exercise.

SOCIALIZATION

A young Pyr that has never been exposed to strangers, traffic noises, or boisterous children could become a confused and frightened adult dog. It is important that a Pyr owner give his or her dog the opportunity to experience all of these situations gradually and with his trusted owner present for support.

Pyr puppies are usually friendly and more than happy to accept strangers, but as they mature, their attitudes can change. They can become reserved and suspicious if the socialization process is neglected. It is absolutely imperative that you continue the socialization process and maintain the pack leader role with your Pyr as he matures.

A well-trained Pyr can serve as a guard dog and a good citizen. A properly trained Pyr knows to obey your commands under all circumstances and that "No!" means just that. Once you give that command, he must stop whatever he is doing and pay attention.

TRAINING Your Great Pyrenees

There is no breed of dog that cannot be trained. Granted, there are some dogs that provide a real challenge, but in most cases, this has more to do with the trainer and his or her training methods than with the dog's inability to learn. Using the proper approach, any dog can be taught to be a good canine citizen. Many dog owners do not understand how a dog learns, nor do they realize they can be breed-specific in their approach to training.

A Great Pyrenees is as smart as his owner allows him to be. It's amazing how quickly puppies can learn! This capacity is greater than most humans realize. However, it is important to remember that these young puppies easily forget what they have learned unless they are constantly reminded.

As puppies leave the nest, they begin their search for two things: a pack leader and the rules by which they can abide. Dog owners often fail miserably in supplying these very basic needs because they immediately begin to respond to the demands of the puppies, and puppies can quickly learn to be very demanding. If a small dog is demanding, he can become a nuisance; if a giant dog, like the Pyr, becomes demanding, he can become uncontrollable.

If a puppy is whining and allowed into the house, he quickly learns that if he makes a fuss, he will get what he wants. Instead of learning the only way he will be fed is to follow a set procedure, such as sitting or lying down on command, the poorly

A good way to curb negative behavior in your dog is to take away things he enjoys, such as a favorite toy or bone.

73

Teaching your Great Pyrenees good manners and obedience skills will ensure that he will become a treasured member of the family for years to come.

educated Pyr puppy learns that leaping about the kitchen and creating a stir is what gets results.

If your Pyr realizes that a growl or a snap can permit him to have his own way, rest assured that the negative behavior will continue or increase. On the other hand, if a dog's unacceptable behavior is met with stern, uncompromising correction, he knows that his behavior does not evoke the desired response.

A good way to help the puppy understand this concept early in life is to take things he enjoys away from him, such as a toy, a bone, or his food dish. If the pup resists, growls, or snaps, correct him firmly and remove the object. Praise him and then return what you have taken away. Everyone in the family must do this with the puppy for it to be effective.

Although you do not have to do this more than once or twice a day, never allow your Pyr puppy to challenge you and have his own way in this situation. You are the pack leader and your puppy depends on you for leadership!

If the young puppy cannot find his pack leader in his owner, he assumes the role of pack leader. If there are no rules imposed, the puppy learns to make his own rules. Unfortunately, the negligent owner continually reinforces the puppy's decisions by allowing him to govern the household.

The key to successful training lies in establishing the proper dog/owner relationship. The owner, or the owning family, must be the pack leader and provide the rules by which the dog abides. This in no way involves cruelty or browbeating your puppy. In fact, your Pyr puppy can and should always be a winner. Even when you deny him certain privileges, like taking away his favorite toy, the pup can be a winner because he is rewarded with a lot of praise when he gives in graciously.

Begin teaching simple lessons like the come command when the puppy is already on his way to you. Do not expect the young puppy to come dashing over to you when he is engrossed in some wonderful adventure. The puppy quickly learns that he will be praised for coming to you on command.

HOUSETRAINING MADE EASY

The recommended method of housetraining is to avoid accidents from happening. The motto is, "Puppies don't make mistakes, people do." A young puppy has no idea what housetraining means; therefore, he can hardly be accused of breaking a rule! *You* must teach the puppy to be an obedient and well-behaved dog by attending to his outdoor needs. Fortunately the Great Pyrenees is very easily housetrained, which is a good thing considering that a mistake from an eight-week-old Pyr puppy looks more like Lake Superior than a puddle! This is not a breed where paper training is an option, because it would take the *New York Times* Sunday edition to soak up just one puddle.

Puppies should go outdoors to relieve themselves after eating, napping, and playing. Carry the puppy outdoors to avoid an accident from occurring on the way. Obviously, you are not going to carry your Pyr puppy for very long, because most Pyr puppies are completely housetrained before they weigh too much to be carried.

Housetraining is a much easier task with the use of a crate. Most breeders use the fiberglass-type or wire crates approved by the airlines for shipping live animals. They are easy to clean and can be used for the dog's entire life.

Some first-time dog owners may see the crate method of housetraining as cruel. What they do not understand is that all dogs need their own places in which to retreat. A puppy will soon look to his crate as his own private den.

Using a crate reduces housetraining time down to an absolute minimum. Begin by feeding your Pyr puppy inside the crate. Keep the door closed and latched while the puppy is eating. When the meal is finished, open the cage and carry the puppy outdoors to the spot where you want him to learn to eliminate. Consistently take your puppy to the same spot to reinforce the habit of going there for that purpose.

It is important that you do not let the puppy run loose after eating. Young puppies will eliminate almost immediately after eating or drinking. They will also be ready to relieve themselves when they first wake up and after playing. If you keep a watchful eye on your puppy, you will quickly learn when he needs to relieve himself. A puppy usually circles and sniffs the floor just before relieving himself.

Do not give your puppy an opportunity to learn that he can eliminate in the house! If an accident occurs, you must correct the puppy while in the act of relieving himself. A puppy does not understand what you are talking about when you reprimand him for something he did minutes before. Reprimand him at the time of the act or not at all. Your housetraining chores will be reduced considerably if you avoid bad habits from beginning in the first place.

If you are not able to watch him every minute, your puppy should be in his crate with the door securely latched. Each time you put your puppy in the crate, give him a small treat of some kind. Throw the treat to the back of the crate and encourage the dog to walk in on his own. When he does so, praise him and hand him another piece of the treat. Understand that a Pyr puppy of 8 to 12 weeks of age will not be able to contain himself for long periods of time. Young puppies must relieve themselves often, except at night. Never leave a very young puppy in a crate for more than four hours during the day. Your schedule must be adjusted accordingly. Also make sure that your puppy has relieved himself at night before the last member of the family retires.

Your first priority in the morning is to get the puppy outdoors. Just how early will depend much more on your puppy than on you. If your Pyr puppy is like most other puppies, there will be no doubt in your mind when he needs to be let out. You will also learn very quickly how to tell the difference between the puppy's

Because of his large size, the Great Pyrenees is easier to housetrain outdoors. In the beginning, you may have to physically carry the puppy outside to avoid an accident from happening.

emergency signals and just unhappy grumbling. Do not test the young puppy's ability to contain himself. The dog's vocal demand to be let out is confirmation that the housetraining lesson is being learned.

BASIC TRAINING

Make sure that you are in the right frame of mind for training sessions. Training should never take place when you are irritated, distressed, or preoccupied. Nor should you begin basic training in crowded or noisy places that will interfere with you or your dog's concentration. Once the commands are understood and learned, you can begin testing your dog in public places, but at first the two of you should work in a place where you can concentrate fully on each other.

The No Command

The most important command your Pyr puppy will ever learn is the meaning of no. The puppy can begin to learn this command the minute he arrives in your home. It is not necessary to frighten the puppy into learning the meaning of the no command, but it is critical that you never give this or any other command you are

Conducting training sessions in a relaxing and open environment that is free of distractions will help your dog stay focused and motivated.

not prepared and able to enforce! The only way a puppy learns to obey commands is to realize that once issued, commands must be complied with.

Leash Training

It is never too early to accustom your Pyr puppy to his leash and collar. The leash and collar is a fail-safe way of keeping your dog under control. It may not be necessary for the puppy or adult Pyr to wear his collar and identification tags within the confines of home, but no dog should ever leave home without a collar and without the leash held securely in his owner's hand.

It is best to begin accustoming your puppy to his collar by leaving a soft collar around his neck

Training your Great Pyr to walk on a leash will give you the chance to enjoy quality time outside together. Be sure to end each lesson with praise.

for a few minutes at a time. Gradually extend the time you leave the collar on. Most Pyr puppies become accustomed to their collars very quickly, and after a few scratches to remove them, forget they are even wearing collars.

While you are playing with the puppy, attach a lightweight leash to the collar. Do not try to guide the puppy at first. The point here is to accustom the puppy to the feeling of having something attached to the collar.

Encourage your puppy to follow you as you move away. If he is reluctant to cooperate, hold a treat in front of the pup's nose to encourage him to follow you. As soon as he takes a few steps toward you, praise him enthusiastically and continue to do so as you continue to move along.

Make the initial session short and fun. Continue the lessons in

Your Pyr puppy must learn to walk on a leash not only for his safety, but for the safety of others as well.

Most dogs have curious natures and like to explore their surroundings; however, their noses don't always lead them to the safest places. Teaching your Great Pyrenees to obey the come command could prevent him from getting into dangerous situations.

your home or yard until your dog is completely unconcerned about the fact that he is on a leash. With a treat in one hand and the leash in the other, you can begin to use both to guide him in the direction you wish to go. Begin your first walks in front of the house and eventually extend them down the street and around the block.

The Come Command

The next most important lesson for the Pyr puppy to learn is to come when called. Therefore it is very important that your puppy learns his name as soon as possible. Constantly repeating the pup's name is what does the trick. Use his name every time you speak to him; for example, "Want to go outside, Rover?" "Come Rover, come!"

Learning to come on command could save your Pyr's life when the two of you venture out into the world. A dog must understand that the come command has to be obeyed without question, but he should not associate that command with fear. Your dog's response to his name and the word come should always be associated with a pleasant experience, such as receiving praise and petting or a food treat.

All too often, novice trainers get very angry at their dogs for not responding immediately to the come command. When the dog finally does come, the owner scolds the dog for not obeying immediately. The dog begins to associate the come command with an unpleasant result. It is much easier to avoid the establishment of bad habits than it is to correct them once set. Avoid giving the come command unless you are sure that your puppy will come to you. The very young puppy is far more inclined to respond to learning the come command than the older dog. Use the command initially when the puppy is already on his way to you or give the command while walking or running away from the youngster. Clap your hands and sound very happy and excited about having the puppy join in on this "game."

The very young Pyr will normally want to stay as close to you as possible, especially in strange surroundings. When your puppy sees you moving away, his natural inclination will be to get close to you. This is a perfect time to use the come command.

Later, as a puppy grows more self-confident and independent, you may want to attach a long leash or rope to his collar to ensure the correct response. Again, do not chase or punish your puppy for not obeying the come command. Doing so in the initial stages of training makes the youngster associate the command with something to fear, and this will result in avoidance rather than the immediate positive response you desire. It is imperative that you praise your puppy and give him a treat when he does come to you, even if he voluntarily delays responding for many minutes.

The Sit and Stay Commands

The sit and stay commands are just as important to your Pyr's safety (and your sanity!) as the no command and learning to come when called. Many Pyr puppies learn the sit command easily, often in just a few minutes, especially if it appears to be a game and a food treat is involved.

Your puppy should always be on collar and leash for his lessons. Young puppies are not beyond getting up and walking away when they have decided that you and your lessons are boring.

Give the sit command immediately before gently pushing down on your puppy's hindquarters or scooping his hind legs under him, molding him into a sit position. Praise your pup lavishly when he

Staying in one place can be very hard for a young puppy. Gently help your Pyr into the sit position if he is having difficulty.

Young puppies will look to their owners for the guidance and discipline they need.

does sit, even though it is you who made the action take place. Again, a food treat always seems to get the lesson across to the youngster.

Continue holding his rear end down and repeat the sit command several times. If he makes an attempt to get up, repeat the command again while exerting light pressure on his rear end until the correct position is assumed. Make your Pyr stay in this position for increasing lengths of time. Begin with a few seconds and increase the time as lessons progress over the following weeks.

If your young student attempts to get up or lie down, simply correct him by saying, "Sit!" in a firm voice. This should be accompanied by returning him to the desired position. Only when *you* decide your dog should get up should he be allowed to do so.

Do not test a very young puppy's patience to the limits. Remember that you are dealing with a baby. The attention span of any youngster, canine or human, is relatively short.

When you do decide that your puppy can get up, call his name, say, "Okay," and make a big fuss over him. Praise and a food treat are in order every time your puppy responds correctly. Continue to help your puppy assume proper positions or respond to commands until he performs on his own. This way a puppy always wins, getting it right every time. You are training with positive reinforcement.

Once your puppy has mastered the sit lesson, you may start on the stay command. With your dog on leash and facing you, command him to sit, then back away a step or two. If the pup attempts to get up to follow, firmly say, "Sit, stay!" While you are saying this, raise your hand, palm toward the dog, and again command, "Stay!"

Any attempt on your dog's part to get up must be corrected at once, returning him to the sit position and repeating, "Stay!" Once your Pyr begins to understand what you want, you can gradually increase the distance you step back. With a long leash attached to his collar (even a clothesline will do), start with a few steps and gradually increase the distance to several yards. Your Pyr will eventually learn the sit and stay command must be obeyed no matter how far away you are. Later on, with advanced training, the dog will learn that the command is to be obeyed even when you move entirely out of sight.

As your Pyr masters this lesson and is able to remain in the sit position for as long as you dictate, avoid calling him *to you* at first. This makes him overly anxious to get up and run to you. Instead, walk back to your dog and say, "Okay," which is the signal that the command is over. Later, when your Pyr becomes more reliable in this respect, you can call him to you.

It is best to keep the stay part of the lesson to a minimum until the puppy is at least five or six months of age. Everything in a very young Pyr's makeup urges him to stay close to you wherever you go. The puppy has bonded to you and forcing him to operate against his natural instincts can be bewildering.

The Down Command

Once your Pyr has mastered the sit and stay commands, you may begin work on the down command, which is the single word

command for lie down. Use the down command *only* when you want the dog to lie down. If you want your dog to get off your sofa or to stop jumping up on people use the off command. Do not interchange these two commands. Doing so will only confuse your dog and evoking the right response will be nearly impossible.

The down position is especially useful if you want your Pyr to remain in a particular place for a long period of time. Usually, a dog is more inclined to stay put when he is lying down than when he is sitting.

Using food treats and praise in conjunction with your training will enable your Great Pyrenees to make positive associations with the basic commands.

Teaching this command to your Pyr may take a little more time and patience than the previous lessons. It is believed by some animal behaviorists that assuming the down position somehow represents submissiveness to the dog. However, as far as Pyr owners are concerned, lying down is the position most Pyrs prefer, and keeping them in the sit position is often more difficult than the down.

With your Pyr sitting in front of and facing you, hold a treat in your right hand with the excess part of the leash in your left hand. Hold the treat under the dog's nose and slowly bring your hand down to the ground. He will follow the treat with his head and neck. As he does, give the command, "Down," and exert *light* pressure on the dog's shoulders with your left hand. If he resists the pressure on his shoulders, do not continue pushing down. Doing so will only create more resistance.

An alternative method of getting your Pyr headed into the down position is to move around to his right side, and, as you draw his attention downward with your right hand, slide your left arm under his front legs and gently slide them forward. Sometimes this is easier to accomplish if you are kneeling.

As your Pyr's forelegs begin to slide out to his front, keep moving the treat along the ground until his whole body is lying on the ground while you continually repeat, "Down." Once your Pyr has assumed the desired position, give the dog a treat and a lot of praise. Continue assisting the pup into the down position until he does so on his own. Be firm and remember that this is a Great Pyrenees, so be patient.

The Heel Command

In learning to heel, your Pyr will walk on your left side with his shoulder next to your leg no matter which direction you might go or how quickly you turn. It is also very important for him to understand this command when the two of you are out walking. Teaching your Pyr to heel will not only make your daily walks far more enjoyable, it will make a far more tractable companion when the two of you are in crowded or confusing situations.

Training your Great Pyrenees to heel will make your daily walks a more relaxing and pleasurable experience.

Many uninformed people are frightened when they see a dog the size of a Pyr coming down the street. A Pyr lunging at the end of the leash, even if it is done to greet the passer-by, can be extremely intimidating.

We have found that a lightweight, link-chain training collar is very useful for the heeling lesson. It provides quick pressure around the neck and a snapping sound, both of which get the dog's attention. Erroneously referred to as a "choke collar," the link-chain collar, when used properly, does not choke the dog.

An employee at the pet shop where you purchase the training collar will be able to show you the proper way to put this collar on your dog. Do not leave this collar on your puppy when training sessions are finished. Because the collar fits loosely, it can get hooked, causing injury or even death. As your puppy grows larger you'll want a sturdier leash as well. We recommend a 6-foot long leash, about three-fourths to one inch wide, made of leather or sturdy nylon.

As you train your puppy to walk along on the leash, you should accustom him to walk on your left side. The leash should cross your body from the dog's collar to your right hand. The excess portion of the leash will be folded into your right hand, and your left hand on the leash will be used to make corrections with the leash.

Training classes are a good way for your Pyr to learn how to get along with other people and dogs.

Performance tests, like tracking, allow dogs to apply their natural talents to the show ring.

A quick short jerk on the leash with your left hand will keep your dog from lunging side to side, pulling ahead, or lagging back. As you make a correction, give the heel command. Keep the leash slack as long as your dog maintains the proper position at your side.

If your dog begins to drift away, give the leash a sharp jerk and guide him back to the correct position and give the heel command. Do not pull on the lead with steady pressure. What is needed is a sharp but gentle jerking motion on the leash to get your dog's attention.

TRAINING CLASSES

There are few limits to what a patient, consistent owner can teach his or her Pyr. For advanced obedience work beyond the basics, however, it is wise for the Pyr owner to consider professional assistance. Professional trainers have had long-standing experience in avoiding the pitfalls of obedience training, and they can help you to avoid these mistakes as well. Pyr owners who have never trained a dog before have found that with professional assistance, their dogs can do very well. This training assistance can be obtained in many ways. Classes are particularly good for your Pyr's socialization. The dog will learn that he must obey his owner even when there are other dogs and people around. These classes also keep the Pyr aware of the fact that he must get along with other people and other dogs.

There are inexpensive classes at many parks and recreation facilities, as well as very formal, and sometimes very expensive, individual lessons with private trainers.

There are also some obedience schools that will train your Pyr for you. A Pyr can and will learn under the care of any professional trainer. However, unless your schedule provides no time at all to train your own dog, having someone else train the dog for you would be last on our list of recommendations. The rapport that develops between the owner who has trained his or her Pyr to be a pleasant companion and good canine citizen is very special, and well worth the time and patience it requires achieving.

FUN AND GAMES

There are many opportunities for you to spend quality time with your Pyr that will provide exercise for you both and valuable training for your dog. In addition to conformation show ring competitions, the AKC and UKC offer obedience classes, agility events, and tracking tests. For the Pyr, there is carting and an endless array of hiking and backpacking activities.

Above all, your Pyr wants to be with you and your family. A Pyr may not always think your ideas are as wonderful as you do, but if you are involved he will do everything possible to go along. Can you ask more of a friend?

SPORT of Purebred Dogs

Welcome to the exciting and sometimes frustrating sport of dogs. No doubt you are trying to learn more about dogs or you wouldn't be deep into this book. This section covers the basics that may entice you, further your knowledge, and help you to understand the dog world.

Dog showing has been a very popular sport for a long time and has been taken quite seriously by some. Others only enjoy it as a hobby.

The Kennel Club in England was formed in 1859, the American Kennel Club was established in 1884, and the Canadian Kennel Club was formed in 1888. The purpose of these clubs was to register purebred dogs and maintain their stud books. In the beginning, the concept of registering dogs was not readily accepted. More than 36 million dogs have been enrolled in the AKC Stud Book since its inception in 1888. Presently, the kennel clubs not only register dogs, but adopt and enforce rules and regulations governing dog shows, obedience trials, and field trials. Over the years they have fostered and encouraged interest in the health and welfare of the purebred dog. They routinely donate funds to veterinary research for study on genetic disorders.

Below are the addresses of the kennel clubs in the United States, Great Britain, and Canada.

The American Kennel Club
260 Madison Avenue
New York, NY 10016
(Their registry is located at: 5580 Centerview Drive, STE 200, Raleigh, NC 27606-3390)

The Kennel Club
1 Clarges Street
Piccadilly, London, WIY 8AB, England

The Canadian Kennel Club
111 Eglinton Avenue
East Toronto, Ontario M6S 4V7
Canada

Successful showing requires dedication and preparation, but most of all, it should be enjoyable for both the dogs and their handlers.

Today there are numerous activities that are enjoyable for both the dog and the handler. Some of the activities include conformation showing, obedience competition, tracking, agility, the Canine Good Citizen® Certificate, and a wide range of instinct tests that vary from breed to breed. Where you start depends upon your goals, which early on may not be readily apparent.

CONFORMATION

Conformation showing is the oldest dog show sport. This type of showing is based on the dog's appearance—that is his structure, movement, and attitude. When considering this type of showing, you need to be aware of your breed's standard and be able to evaluate your dog compared to that standard. The breeder of your puppy or other experienced breeders would be good sources for such an evaluation. Puppies can go through lots of changes over a period of time. Many puppies start out as promising hopefuls and then after maturing may be disappointing as show candidates. Even so, this should not deter them from being excellent pets.

Conformation training classes are usually offered by the local kennel or obedience clubs. These are excellent places for training puppies. The puppy should be able to walk on a lead before entering such a class. Proper ring procedure and technique for posing (stacking) the dog will be demonstrated, as well as gaiting the dog. Generally, certain patterns are used in the ring, such as the triangle or the "L." Conformation class, like the PKT class, will give your youngster the opportunity to socialize with different breeds of dog and humans, too.

It takes some time to learn the routine of conformation showing. Usually, one starts at the puppy matches that may be AKC sanctioned or fun matches. These matches are generally for puppies from 2 or 3 months to a year old, and there may be classes for the adult over the age of 12 months. Similar to point shows, the classes are divided by sex, and after completion of the classes in that breed or variety, the class winners compete for Best of Breed or Variety. The winner goes on to compete in the Group, and the Group winners compete for Best in Match. No championship points are awarded for match wins.

In conformation showing, your Great Pyrenees will be judged on his appearance, including his structure, movement, and attitude.

Match shows can be a great place for puppies to learn socialization skills and meet new people.

A few matches can be great training for puppies, even if there is no intention to go on showing. Matches enable the puppy to meet new people and be handled by a stranger—the judge. It also offers a change of environment, which broadens the horizon for both dog and handler. Matches and other dog activities boost the confidence of the handler, and especially the younger handlers.

Earning an AKC championship is built on a point system, which is different from Great Britain. To become an AKC Champion of Record, the dog must earn 15 points. The number of points earned each time depends upon the number of dogs in competition. The number of points available at each show depends upon the breed, its sex, and the location of the show. The United States is divided into ten AKC zones. Each zone has its own set of points. The purpose of the zones is to try to equalize the points available from breed to breed and area to area. The AKC adjusts the point scale annually.

The number of points that can be won at a show are between one and five. Three-, four- and five-point wins are considered majors. Not only does the dog need 15 points won under 3 different judges, but those points must include 2 majors under 2 different judges. Canada also works on a point system, but majors are not required.

Dogs always show before bitches. The classes available to those seeking points are: Puppy (which may be divided into 6 to 9 months and 9 to 12 months); 12 to 18 months; Novice; Bred-by-Exhibitor; American-bred; and Open. The class winners of the same sex of each breed or variety compete against each other for Winners Dog and Winners Bitch. A Reserve Winners Dog and Reserve Winners Bitch are also awarded but do not carry any points unless the Winners win is disallowed by AKC. The Winners Dog and Bitch compete with the Specials (those dogs that have attained championship) for Best of Breed or Variety, Best of Winners, and Best of Opposite Sex. It is possible to pick up an extra point or even a major if the points are higher for the defeated winner than those of Best of Winners. The latter would get the higher total from the defeated winner.

At an all-breed show, each Best of Breed or Variety winner will go on to his respective Group and then the Group winners will compete against each other for Best in Show. There are seven Groups: Sporting, Hounds, Working, Terriers, Toys, Non-Sporting, and Herding. Obviously, there are no Groups at speciality shows (those shows that have only one breed or a show such as the American Spaniel Club's Flushing Spaniel Show, which is for all flushing spaniel breeds).

Earning a championship in England is somewhat different since they do not have a point system. Challenge Certificates are awarded if the judge feels the dog is deserving, regardless of the number of dogs in competition. A dog must earn 3 Challenge Certificates under 3 different judges, with at least 1 of these Certificates being won after the age of 12 months. Competition is very strong and entries may be higher than they are in the US. The Kennel Club's Challenge Certificates are only available at championship shows.

In England, The Kennel Club regulations require that certain dogs, Border Collies and gundog breeds, qualify in a working capacity (i.e., obedience or field trials) before becoming a full champion. If they do not qualify in the working aspect, then they are designated a show champion, which is equivalent to the AKC's Champion of Record. A gundog may be granted the title of Field Trial Champion (FTCh.) if it passes all the tests in the field, but would also have to qualify in conformation before becoming a full champion. A Border Collie that earns the title of Obedience Champion (ObCh.) must also qualify in the conformation ring before becoming a champion.

The US doesn't have a designation full Champion, but does award for Dual and Triple Champions. The Dual Champion must be a Champion of Record, and either Champion Tracker, Herding Champion, Obedience Trial Champion, or Field Champion. Any dog that has been awarded the titles of Champion of Record, and any two of the following: Champion Tracker, Herding Champion, Obedience Trial Champion or Field Champion, may be designated as a Triple Champion.

The shows in England seem to put more emphasis on breeder judges than those in the US. There is much competition within the breeds. Therefore, the quality of the individual breeds should be very good. In the US we tend to have more "all around judges," (those that judge multiple breeds) and use the breeder judges at the specialty shows. Breeder judges are more familiar with their own breed as they are actively breeding that breed or did so at one time. Americans emphasize Group and Best in Show wins and promote them accordingly.

The shows in England can be very large and extend over several days, with the Groups being scheduled on different days. Though multi-day shows are not common in the U.S., there are cluster shows in which several different clubs will use the same show site over consecutive days.

Westminster Kennel Club is our most prestigious show, although the entry is limited to 2500. In recent years, entry has been limited to champions. This show is more formal than the majority of the shows, with the judges wearing formal attire and the handlers fashionably dressed. In most instances, the quality of the dogs is superb. After all, it is a show of champions. It is a good show to study the AKC registered breeds and is by far the most exciting—especially since it is televised! WKC is one of the few shows in this country that is still benched. This means the dog must be in his benched area during the show hours, except when he is being groomed, is in the ring, or is being exercised.

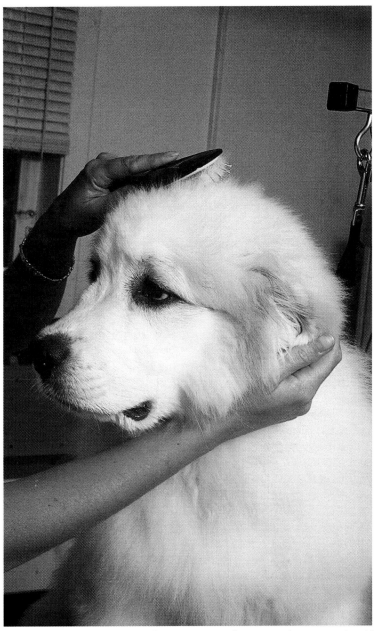

Your Great Pyrenees must be accustomed to extensive grooming if he is going to compete in the show ring.

Typically, the handlers are very particular about their appearances. They are careful not to wear something that will detract from their dogs but will perhaps enhance them. American ring procedure is quite formal compared to that of other countries. There is a certain etiquette expected between the judge and exhibitor and among the other exhibitors. Of course, it is not always the case, but the judge is supposed to be polite, not engaging in small talk or acknowledging how well he knows the handler. There is a more informal and relaxed atmosphere at the shows in other countries. For instance, the dress code is more casual. I can see where this might be more fun for the exhibitor and especially for the novice. The US is very handler-oriented in many of the breeds. It is true, in most instances, that the experienced professional handler can better present the dog and will have a feel for what a judge likes.

In England, Crufts is The Kennel Club's own show and is most assuredly the largest dog show in the world. It's been known to have an entry of nearly 20,000, and the show lasts four days. Entry is only gained by qualifying through winning in specified classes at another championship show. Westminster is strictly conformation, but Crufts exhibitors and spectators enjoy not only conformation but obedience, agility, and a multitude of exhibitions, as well. Obedience was admitted in 1957 and agility in 1983.

If you are handling your own dog, please give some consideration to your apparel. The dress code at matches is more informal than at the point shows. However, you should wear something a little more appropriate than beach attire or ragged jeans and bare feet. If you check out the handlers and see what is presently fashionable, you'll catch on. Men usually dress with a shirt and tie and a nice sports coat. Whether you are male or female, you will want to wear comfortable clothes and shoes. You need to be able to run with your dog, and you certainly don't want to take a chance of falling and hurting yourself. Heaven forbid, if nothing else, you'll upset your dog. Women usually wear a dress or two-piece outfit, preferably with pockets to carry bait, brush, etc. In this case, men are the lucky ones with all their pockets. Ladies, think about where your dress will be if you need to kneel on the floor, and also think about running. Does it allow freedom to do so?

A grooming table is just one of the many pieces of equipment you will need to bring with you to a dog show.

You need to take along dog; crate; ex pen (if you use one); extra bedding; water pail and water; all required grooming equipment; table; chair for you; bait for dog and lunch for you and friends; and, last but not least, clean up materials, such as plastic bags, paper towels, and perhaps a bath towel and some shampoo—just in case. Don't forget your entry confirmation and directions to the show.

If you are showing in obedience, you may want to wear pants. Many of our top obedience handlers wear pants that are color-coordinated with their dogs. The philosophy is that imperfections in the black dog will be less obvious next to your black pants.

Whether you are showing in conformation, Junior Showmanship, or obedience, you need to watch the clock and be sure you are not late. It is customary to pick up your conformation armband a few minutes before the start of the class. They will not wait for you, and if you are on the show grounds and not in the ring, you will upset everyone. It's a little more complicated picking up your obedience armband if you show later in the class. If you have not picked it up and they get to your number, you may not be allowed to show. It's best to pick up your armband early, but be aware that you may show earlier than expected if other handlers don't pick up. Customarily, all conflicts should be discussed with the judge prior to the start of the class.

Junior Showmanship

The Junior Showmanship Class is a wonderful way to build self confidence, even if there are no aspirations of staying with the dog-show game later in life. Frequently, Junior Showmanship becomes the background of those who become successful exhibitors/handlers in the future. In some instances, it is taken very seriously, and success is measured in terms of wins. The Junior Handler is judged solely on his ability and skill in presenting his dog. The dog's conformation is not to be considered by the judge. Even so, the condition and grooming of the dog may be a reflection upon the handler.

Usually, the matches and point shows include different classes. The Junior Handler's dog may be entered in a breed or obedience class and even shown by another person in that class. Junior Showmanship classes are usually divided by age and perhaps sex. The age is determined by the handler's age on the day of the show. The classes are:

Novice Junior for those at least 10 and under 14 years of age, who at time of entry closing have not won 3 first places in a Novice Class at a licensed or member show.

Novice Senior for those at least 14 and under 18 years of age, who at the time of entry closing have not won 3 first places in a Novice Class at a licensed or member show.

Open Junior for those at least 10 and under 14 years of age, who at the time of entry closing have won at least 3 first places in a Novice Junior Showmanship Class at a licensed or member show with competition present.

Open Senior for those at least 14 and under 18 years of age, who at time of entry closing have won at least 3 first places in a Novice Junior Showmanship Class at a licensed or member show with competition present.

Junior Handlers must include their AKC Junior Handler number on each show entry. This needs to be obtained from the AKC.

CANINE GOOD CITIZEN®

The AKC sponsors a program to encourage dog owners to train their dogs. Local clubs perform the pass/fail tests, and dogs that

Socializing your Great Pyrenees with other animals and people at a young age will benefit him later in life. A well-socialized and friendly dog is a perfect candidate to become a Canine Good Citizen.

pass are awarded a Canine Good Citizen® Certificate. Proof of vaccination is required at the time of participation. The test includes:

1. Accepting a friendly stranger.
2. Sitting politely for petting.
3. Appearance and grooming.
4. Walking on a loose leash.
5. Walking through a crowd.
6. Sit and down on command/staying in place.
7. Come when called.
8. Reaction to another dog.
9. Reactions to distractions.
10. Supervised separation.

If more effort was made by pet owners to accomplish these exercises, fewer dogs would be cast off to the humane shelter.

The versatile Great Pyrenees can compete in many different events, including obedience and herding trials.

OBEDIENCE

Obedience is necessary, without a doubt, but it can also become a wonderful hobby or even an obsession. Obedience classes and competition can provide wonderful companionship, not only with your dog but with your classmates or fellow competitors. It is always gratifying to discuss your dog's problems with others who have had similar experiences. The AKC acknowledged obedience around 1936, and it has changed tremendously even though many of the exercises are basically the same. Today, obedience competition is just that—very competitive. Even so, it is possible for every obedience exhibitor to come home a winner (by earning qualifying scores), even though he/she may not earn a placement in the class.

Most of the obedience titles are awarded after earning three qualifying scores (legs) in the appropriate class under three different judges. These classes offer a perfect score of 200, which is extremely rare. Each of the class exercises has its own point value. A leg is earned after receiving a score of at least 170 and at least 50 percent of the points available in each exercise. The titles are:

Companion Dog–CD
This is called the Novice Class and the exercises are:

1. Heel on leash and figure 8	40 points
2. Stand for examination	30 points
3. Heel free	40 points
4. Recall	30 points
5. Long sit–one minute	30 points
6. Long down–three minutes	30 points
Maximum total score	200 points

Companion Dog Excellent–CDX
This is the Open Class and the exercises are:

1. Heel off leash and figure 8	40 points
2. Drop on recall	30 points
3. Retrieve on flat	20 points
4. Retrieve over high jump	30 points
5. Broad jump	20 points
6. Long sit–three minutes (out of sight)	30 points
7. Long down–five minutes (out of sight)	30 points
Maximum total score	200 points

Utility Dog–UD

The Utility Class exercises are:

1. Signal exercise	40 points
2. Scent discrimination-Article 1	30 points
3. Scent discrimination-Article 2	30 points
4. Directed retrieve	30 points
5. Moving stand and examination	30 points
6. Directed jumping	40 points
Maximum total score	200 points

After achieving the UD title, you may feel inclined to go after the UDX and/or OTCh. The UDX (Utility Dog Excellent) title went into effect in January 1994. It is not easily attained. The title requires qualifying simultaneously ten times in Open B and Utility B, but not necessarily at consecutive shows.

The OTCh. (Obedience Trial Champion) is awarded after the dog has earned his UD and then goes on to earn 100 championship points, a first place in Utility, a first place in Open, and another first place in either class. The placements must be won under three different judges at all-breed obedience trials. The points are determined by the number of dogs competing in the Open B and Utility B classes. The OTCh. title precedes the dog's name.

Obedience matches (AKC-sanctioned, fun, and show and go) are often available. Usually, they are sponsored by the local obedience clubs. When preparing an obedience dog for a title, you will find matches very helpful. Fun matches and show and go matches are more lenient in allowing you to make corrections in the ring. This type of training is usually very necessary for the Open and Utility classes. AKC-sanctioned obedience matches do not allow corrections in the ring since they must abide by the AKC obedience regulations booklet. If you are interested in showing in obedience, then you should contact the AKC for a copy of *Obedience Regulations.*

TRACKING

Tracking is officially classified as obedience. There are three tracking titles available: Tracking Dog (TD), Tracking Dog Excellent (TDX), and Variable Surface Tracking (VST). If all three tracking titles are obtained, then the dog officially becomes a CT (Champion Tracker). The CT will go in front of the dog's name.

A TD may be earned anytime and does not have to follow the other obedience titles. There are many exhibitors that prefer tracking to obedience, and there are others who do both.

Tracking Dog—TD

A dog must be certified by an AKC tracking judge that he is ready to perform in an AKC test. The AKC can provide the names of tracking judges in your area that you can contact for certification. Depending on where you live, you may have to travel a distance if there is no local tracking judge nearby. The certification track will be equivalent to a regular AKC track. A regulation track must be 440 to 500 yards long, with at least two right-angle turns out in the open. The track will be aged 30 minutes to 2 hours. The handler has two starting flags at the beginning of the track to indicate the direction started. The dog works on a harness and 40-foot lead and must work at least 20 feet in front of the handler. An article (either a dark glove or wallet) will be dropped at the end of the track, and the dog must indicate it but not necessarily retrieve it.

People always ask what the dog tracks. Initially, the beginner on the short-aged track tracks the tracklayer. Eventually, the dog learns to track the disturbed vegetation and learns to differentiate between tracks. Getting started with tracking requires reading the AKC regulations and a good book on tracking, plus finding other tracking enthusiasts. Work on the buddy system. That is, lay tracks for each other so you can practice blind tracks. It is possible to train on your own, but if you are a beginner, it is a lot more entertaining to track with a buddy. It's rewarding seeing the dog use his natural ability.

Tracking Dog Excellent—TDX

The TDX track is 800 to 1000 yards long and is aged 3 to 5 hours. There will be five to seven turns. An article is left at the starting flag, and three other articles must be indicated on the track. There is only one flag at the start, so it is a blind start. Approximately one and a half hours after the track is laid, two tracklayers will cross over the track at two different places to test the dog's ability to stay with the original track. There will be at least two obstacles on the track, such as a change of cover, fences, creeks, ditches, etc. The dog must have a TD before entering a TDX. There is no certification required for a TDX.

Herding competitions are a great place for your Great Pyrenees to show off his considerable skills and to be recognized for his special talents.

Variable Surface Tracking–VST

This test came into effect in September 1995. The dog must have a TD earned at least six months prior to entering this test. The track is 600 to 800 yards long and shall have a minimum of 3 different surfaces. Vegetation shall be included along with two areas devoid of vegetation, such as concrete, asphalt, gravel, sand, hard pan, or mulch. The areas devoid of vegetation shall comprise at least one-third to one-half of the track. The track is aged three to five hours. There will be four to eight turns and four numbered articles, including one leather, one plastic, one metal, and one fabric dropped on the track. There is one starting flag. The handler will work at least ten feet from the dog.

General Information

Obedience, tracking, and agility allow the purebred dog with an Indefinite Listing Privilege (ILP) number or a limited registration to be exhibited and earn titles. Application must be made to the AKC for an ILP number.

The American Kennel Club publishes *Events*, a monthly magazine that is part of the *Gazette*, their official journal for the sport of purebred dogs. The *Events* section lists upcoming shows and the secretary or superintendent for them. The majority of the conformation shows in the US are overseen by licensed superintendents. Generally, the entry closing date is approximately two-and-a-half weeks before the actual show. Point shows are fairly expensive, while the match shows cost about one-third of the point show entry fee. Match shows usually take entries the day of the show, but some are pre-entry. The best way to find match show information is through your local kennel club. Upon asking, the AKC can provide you with a list of superintendents, and you can write and ask to be put on their mailing lists.

Obedience trial and tracking test information is also available through the AKC. Frequently, these events are not superintended, but put on by the host club. Therefore, you would make the entry with the event's secretary.

There are numerous activities you can share with your dog. Regardless of what you do, it does take teamwork. Your dog can only benefit from your attention and training. We hope this chapter has enlightened you and hope, if nothing else, you will attend a show here and there. Perhaps you will start with a puppy kindergarten class, and who knows where it may lead!

HEALTH CARE

Veterinary medicine has become far more sophisticated than what was available to our ancestors. This can be attributed to the increase in household pets and, consequently, the demand for better care for them. Also human medicine has become far more complex. Today, diagnostic testing in veterinary medicine parallels human diagnostics. Because of better technology, we can expect our pets to live healthier lives, thereby increasing their life spans.

THE FIRST CHECKUP

You will want to take your new puppy/dog in for his first check up within 48 to 72 hours after acquiring him. Many breeders strongly recommend this checkup and so do the humane shelters. A puppy/dog can appear healthy, but he may have a serious problem that is not apparent to the layman. Most pets have some type of a minor flaw that may never cause a real problem.

Young puppies are very vulnerable to diseases. Responsible pet owners should take every precaution to keep their pups healthy and protected.

The antibodies that puppies receive from their mother's milk will protect them from disease for the first few weeks of life. Because the antibodies are only temporarily effective, vaccinations are necessary.

Unfortunately, if he/she should have a serious problem, you will want to consider the consequences of keeping the pet and the attachments that will be formed, which may be broken prematurely. Keep in mind there are many healthy dogs looking for good homes.

This first checkup is a good time to establish yourself with the veterinarian and to learn the office policy regarding their hours and how they handle emergencies. Usually, the breeder or another conscientious pet owner is a good reference for locating a capable veterinarian. You should be aware that not all vets give the same quality of service. Please do not make your selection based on the least expensive clinic, as they may be short changing your pet. There is the possibility that it will eventually cost you more due to improper diagnosis, treatment, etc. If you are selecting a new veterinarian, feel free to ask for a tour of the clinic. You should inquire about making an appointment for a tour, because all clinics are working clinics, and therefore, may not be available all day for sightseers. You may worry less if you see where your pet will be spending the day if he ever needs to be hospitalized.

THE PHYSICAL EXAM

Your veterinarian will check your pet's overall condition, which includes listening to the heart; checking the respiration; feeling the abdomen, muscles, and joints; checking the mouth, which includes gum color and signs of gum disease, along with plaque buildup; checking the ears for signs of an infection or ear mites; examining the eyes; and, last but not least, checking the condition of the skin and coat.

He should ask you questions regarding your pet's eating and elimination habits and invite you to relay your questions. It is a good idea to prepare a list so as not to forget anything. He should discuss the proper diet and the quantity to be fed. If this differs from your breeder's recommendation, you should convey to him what the breeder's choice is and see if he approves. If he recommends changing the diet, this should be done over a few days so as not to cause a gastrointestinal upset. It is customary to take in a fresh stool sample (just a small amount) to test for intestinal parasites. It must be fresh, preferably within 12 hours, because the eggs hatch quickly and after hatching will not be observed under the microscope. If your pet isn't obliging then, the technician can usually take a sample in the clinic.

IMMUNIZATIONS

It is important that you take your puppy/dog's vaccination record with you on your first visit. In the case of a puppy, presumably the breeder has seen to the vaccinations up to the time you acquired custody. Veterinarians differ in their vaccination protocol. It is not unusual for your puppy to have received vaccinations for distemper, hepatitis, leptospirosis, parvovirus, and parainfluenza every two to three weeks from the age of five or six weeks. Usually, this is a combined injection and is typically called the DHLPP. The DHLPP is given through at least 12 to 14 weeks of age, and it is customary to continue with another parvovirus vaccine at 16 to 18 weeks. You may wonder why so many immunizations are necessary. No one knows for sure when the puppy's maternal antibodies are gone, although it is customarily accepted that distemper antibodies are gone by 12 weeks. Usually, parvovirus antibodies are gone by 16 to 18 weeks of age. However, it is possible for the maternal antibodies to be gone much earlier

Maintaining your puppy's immunization schedule and booster shots will increase the longevity of his life.

or even at a later age. Therefore, immunizations are started at an early age. The vaccine will not give immunity as long as there are maternal antibodies. The rabies vaccination is given at three or six months of age, depending on your local laws. A vaccine for bordetella (kennel cough) is advisable and can be given any time from the age of five weeks. The coronavirus is not commonly given unless there is a problem locally. The Lyme vaccine is necessary in endemic areas. Lyme disease has been reported in 47 states.

Distemper

Distemper is virtually an incurable disease. If the dog recovers, he is subject to severe nervous disorders. The virus attacks every tissue in the body and resembles a bad cold with a fever. It can cause a runny nose and eyes and cause gastrointestinal disorders, including a poor appetite, vomiting, and diarrhea. The virus is carried by raccoons, foxes, wolves, mink, and other dogs. Unvaccinated youngsters and senior citizens are very susceptible. This is still a common disease.

Hepatitis

Hepatitis is a virus that is most serious in very young dogs. It is spread by contact with an infected animal or its stool or urine. The virus affects the liver and kidneys and is characterized by high fever, depression, and lack of appetite. Recovered animals may be afflicted with chronic illnesses.

Leptospirosis

Leptospirosis is a bacterial disease transmitted by contact with the urine of an infected dog, rat, or other wildlife. It produces severe symptoms of fever, depression, jaundice, and internal bleeding and was fatal before the vaccine was developed. Recovered dogs can be carriers, and the disease can be transmitted from dogs to humans.

Parvovirus

Parvovirus was first noted in the late 1970s and is still a fatal disease. However, with proper vaccinations, early diagnosis, and prompt treatment, it is a manageable disease. It attacks the bone marrow and intestinal tract. The symptoms include depression, loss of appetite, vomiting, diarrhea, and collapse. Immediate medical attention is of the essence.

Rabies

Rabies is shed in the saliva and is carried by raccoons, skunks, foxes, other dogs, and cats. It attacks nerve tissue, resulting in paralysis and death. Rabies can be transmitted to people and is virtually always fatal. This disease is reappearing in the suburbs.

Bordetella (Kennel Cough)

The symptoms of bordetella are coughing, sneezing, hacking, and retching accompanied by nasal discharge usually lasting from a few days to several weeks. There are several disease-producing organisms responsible for this disease.

Bordetella attached to canine cilia. Otherwise known as kennel cough, this highly contagious disease should be vaccinated against.

The present vaccines are helpful but do not protect for all the strains. It usually is not life threatening, but in some instances it can progress to a serious bronchopneumonia. The disease is highly contagious. The vaccination should be given routinely for dogs that come into contact with other dogs, such as through boarding, training class, or visits to the groomer.

Coronavirus

Coronavirus is usually self-limiting and not a life-threatening disease. It was first noted in the late '70s about a year before parvovirus. The virus produces a yellow/brown stool, and there may be depression, vomiting, and diarrhea.

Lyme Disease

Lyme disease was first diagnosed in the United States in 1976 in Lyme, CT, in people who lived in close proximity to the deer tick. Symptoms may include acute lameness, fever, swelling of joints, and loss of appetite. Your veterinarian can advise you if you live in an endemic area.

Booster Shots

After your puppy has completed his puppy vaccinations, you will continue to booster the DHLPP once a year. It is customary to booster the rabies one year after the first vaccine and then, depending on where you live, it should be boostered every year or every three years. This depends on your local laws. The Lyme and corona vaccines are boostered annually, and it is recommended that the bordetella be boostered every six to eight months.

ANNUAL VISIT

I would like to impress the importance of the annual checkup, which would include booster vaccinations, a check for intestinal parasites, and a test for heartworm. Today, in our very busy world, it is rush, rush, and see "how much you can get for how little." Unbelievably, some nonveterinary establishments have entered into the vaccination business. More harm than good can come to your dog through improper vaccinations, possibly from inferior vaccines and/or the wrong schedule. More than likely, you truly care about your companion dog, and over the years you have devoted much time and expense to his well being. Perhaps you are unaware that a vaccination is not just a vaccination. There is

Parasites can be transmitted to your puppy via other dogs. Make sure that your Great Pyrenees has received the proper immunizations before taking him out to make new friends.

more involved. Please follow through with regular physical examinations. It is so important for your veterinarian to know your dog, and this is especially true during middle age and through the geriatric years. Your older dog may require more than one physical a year. The annual physical is good preventive medicine. Through early diagnosis and subsequent treatment, your dog can maintain a longer and better quality of life.

INTESTINAL PARASITES

Hookworms

A young puppy is very vulnerable to disease and germs. Take your Great Pyrenees puppy to the vet within 48 to 72 hours after acquiring him. He should also have regular checkups throughout his lifetime to maintain good health.

Hookworms are almost microscopic intestinal worms that can cause anemia and, therefore, serious problems, including death, in young puppies. Hookworms can be transmitted to humans through penetration of the skin. Puppies may be born with them.

Roundworms

Roundworms are spaghetti-like worms that can cause a potbellied appearance and dull coat, along with more severe symptoms such as vomiting, diarrhea, and coughing. Puppies acquire these while in the mother's uterus and through lactation. Both hookworms and roundworms may be acquired through ingestion.

Whipworms

Whipworms have a three-month life cycle and are not acquired through the dam. They cause intermittent diarrhea, usually with mucus. Whipworms are possibly the most difficult worm to

Keeping stray dogs out of your yard helps your Great Pyrenees from contracting intestinal parasites.

eradicate. Their eggs are very resistant to most environmental factors and can last for years until the proper conditions enable them to mature. Whipworms are seldom seen in the stool.

Intestinal parasites are more prevalent in some areas than others. Climate, soil, and contamination are big factors contributing to the incidence of intestinal parasites. Eggs are passed in the stool, lay on the ground, and then become infective in a certain number of days. Each of the above worms has a different life cycle. Your dog's best chance of becoming and remaining worm-free is to always pooper-scoop your yard. A fenced-in yard keeps stray dogs out, which is certainly helpful.

Having a fecal examination done on your dog twice a year, or more often if there is a problem, is recommended. If your dog has a positive fecal sample, he will be given the appropriate medication and you will be asked to bring back another stool sample in a certain period of time (depending on the type of worm), and then he will be rewormed. This process goes on until he has at least two negative samples. Different types of worm require different medications. You will be wasting your money and doing your dog an injustice by buying over-the-counter medication without first consulting your veterinarian.

OTHER INTERNAL PARASITES

Coccidiosis and Giardiasis

Coccidiosis and giardiasis, which are protozoal infections, usually affect pups, especially in places where large numbers of puppies are brought together. Older dogs may harbor these infections, but do not show signs unless they are stressed. Symptoms include diarrhea, weight loss and lack of appetite. These infections are not always apparent in the fecal examination.

Tapeworms

Seldom apparent on fecal floatation, tapeworms are diagnosed frequently as rice-like segments around the dog's anus and the base of the tail. Tapeworms are long, flat, and ribbon-like, sometimes several feet in length, and made up of many segments about five-eighths of an inch long. The two most common causes of tapeworm found in the dog are:

(1) The larval form of the flea tapeworm parasite matures in an intermediate host, the flea, before it can become infective. Your dog acquires this by ingesting the flea through licking and chewing.

(2) Rabbits, rodents, and certain large game animals serve as intermediate hosts for other species of tapeworm. If your dog eats one of these infected hosts, he can acquire tapeworms.

HEARTWORM DISEASE

Heartworm is a worm that resides in the heart and adjacent blood vessels of the lung that produces microfilaria, which circulate in the bloodstream. It is possible for a dog to be infected

The importance of consulting a vet on the diagnosis of internal disorders cannot be stressed enough—a relatively common problem could also be a sign of something more serious.

There are many parasites, like fleas and ticks, that your Great Pyrenees may encounter while playing outside. Be sure to check his coat thoroughly when he comes in from the outdoors.

with any number of worms from one to a hundred that can be 6 to 14 inches long. It is a life-threatening disease, expensive to treat, and easily prevented. Depending on where you live, your veterinarian may recommend a preventive year-round and either an annual or semiannual blood test. The most common preventive is given once a month.

EXTERNAL PARASITES

Fleas

Fleas are not only the dog's worst enemy, but also enemy to the owner's pocketbook. Preventing is less expensive than treating, but regardless, we'd prefer to spend our money elsewhere. Likely, the majority of our dogs are allergic to the bite of a flea, and in many cases, it only takes one flea bite. The protein in the flea's saliva is the culprit. Allergic dogs have a reaction, which usually results in a "hot spot." More than likely, such a reaction will involve a trip to the veterinarian for treatment. Yes, prevention is less expensive. Fortunately, today there are several good products available.

Regular physical exams are vital to the health and long life of your canine companion.

If there is a flea infestation, no one product is going to correct the problem. Not only will the dog require treatment, so will the environment. In general, flea collars are not very effective although there is an "egg" collar now available that will kill the eggs on the dog. Dips are the most economical, but they are messy. There are some effective shampoos and treatments available through pet shops and veterinarians. An oral tablet arrived on the American market in 1995 and was popular in Europe the previous year. It sterilizes the female flea, but will not kill adult fleas. Therefore, the tablet, which is given monthly, will decrease the flea population but is not a "cure-all." Those dogs that suffer from flea-bite allergy will still be subjected to the bite of the flea. Another popular parasiticide is permethrin, which is applied to the back of the dog in one or two places, depending on the dog's weight. This product works as a repellent, causing the flea to get "hot feet" and jump off. Do not confuse this product with some of the organophosphates that are also applied to the dog's back.

Some products are not usable on young puppies. Treating fleas should be done under your veterinarian's guidance. Frequently, it is necessary to combine products, and the layman does not have knowledge regarding possible toxicities. It is hard to believe, but there are a few dogs that do have a natural resistance to fleas. Nevertheless, it would be wise to treat all pets at the same time. Don't forget your cats. Cats just love to prowl the neighborhood, and, consequently, return with unwanted guests.

Adult fleas live on the dog, but their eggs drop off into the environment. There, they go through four larval stages before reaching adulthood, and thereby are able to jump back on the poor unsuspecting dog. The cycle resumes and takes between 21 to 28 days under ideal conditions. There are environmental products available that will kill both adult fleas and larvae.

Ticks

Ticks can carry Rocky Mountain Spotted Fever, Lyme disease, and can cause tick paralysis. They should be removed with tweezers. Try to pull out the head because the jaws carry disease. There is a tick preventive collar that does an excellent job. The ticks automatically back out on those dogs wearing collars.

Sarcoptic Mange

Sarcoptic mange is a mite that is difficult to find on skin scrapings. The pinnal reflex is a good indicator of this disease. Rub the ends of the pinna (ear) together and the dog will start scratching with his foot. Sarcoptes are highly contagious to other dogs and to humans, although they do not live long on humans. They cause intense itching.

Demodectic Mange

Demodectic mange is a mite that is passed from the dam to her puppies. It affects youngsters aged three to ten months. Diagnosis is confirmed by skin scraping. Small areas of alopecia around the eyes, lips, and/or forelegs become visible. There is little itching, unless there is a secondary bacterial infection. Some breeds are afflicted more than others.

Cheyletiella

Cheyletiella causes intense itching and is diagnosed by skin scraping. It lives in the outer layers of the skin of dogs, cats, rabbits, and humans. Yellow-gray scales may be found on the back and the rump, top of the head, and the nose.

Breeding requires a great amount of knowledge about the breed and should not be taken lightly, so most breeders will ask that you have your pet spayed or neutered.

Breeding only the best-quality dogs ensures that the Great Pyrenees will stay free of hereditary diseases.

TO BREED OR NOT TO BREED

More than likely, your breeder has requested that you have your puppy neutered or spayed. Your breeder's request is based on what is healthiest for your dog and what is most beneficial for your breed. Experienced and conscientious breeders devote many years to developing a bloodline. In order to do this, they make every effort to plan each breeding in regard to conformation, temperament, and health. This type of breeder does his best to perform the necessary testing (i.e., OFA, CERF, testing for inherited blood disorders, thyroid, etc.). Testing is expensive and sometimes very disheartening when a favorite dog doesn't pass his health tests. The health history pertains not only to the breeding stock, but to the immediate ancestors. Reputable breeders do not want their offspring to be bred indiscriminately. Therefore, you may be asked to neuter or spay your puppy. Of course, there is always the exception, and the breeder may agree to let you breed your dog under his direct supervision. This is an important concept. More and more effort is being made to breed healthier dogs.

Spay/Neuter

There are numerous benefits to spaying or neutering your dog at six months of age. Unspayed females are subject to mammary and ovarian cancer. In order to prevent mammary cancer, she must be spayed prior to her first heat cycle. Later in life, an unspayed female may develop a pyometra (an infected uterus), which is definitely life threatening.

Spaying is performed under a general anesthetic and is easy on the young dog. As you might expect, it is a little harder on the older dog, but that is no reason to deny her the surgery. The surgery removes the ovaries and uterus. It is important to remove all the ovarian tissue. If some is left behind, she could remain attractive to males. In order to view the ovaries, a reasonably long incision is necessary. An ovariohysterectomy is considered major surgery.

Neutering the male at a young age will inhibit some characteristic male behavior that owners frown upon. Some boys will not hike their legs and mark territory if they are neutered at six months of age. Also, neutering at a young age has hormonal benefits, lessening the chance of hormonal aggressiveness.

Surgery involves removing the testicles but leaving the scrotum. If there should be a retained testicle, the male definitely needs to be neutered before the age of two or three years. Retained testicles can develop cancer. Unneutered males are at risk for testicular cancer, perineal fistulas, perianal tumors, and fistulas and prostatic disease.

Intact males and females are prone to housetraining accidents. Females urinate frequently before, during, and after heat cycles, and males tend to mark territory if there is a female in heat. Males may show the same behavior if there is a visiting dog or guests.

Surgery involves a sterile operating procedure equivalent to human surgery. The incision site is shaved, surgically scrubbed, and draped. The veterinarian wears a sterile surgical gown, cap, mask, and gloves. Anesthesia should be monitored by a registered technician. It is customary for the veterinarian to recommend a pre-anesthetic blood screening, looking for metabolic problems, and a ECG rhythm strip to check for normal heart function. Today, anesthetics are equal to human anesthetics, which enables your dog to walk out of the clinic the same day as surgery. Some folks worry about their dogs gaining weight after being neutered or spayed. This is usually not the case. It is true that some dogs may be less active so they could develop a problem, but most are just as active as they were before surgery. However, if your dog should begin to gain, you need to decrease his food and see to it that he gets a little more exercise.

MEDICAL PROBLEMS

Anal Sacs

Anal sacs are small sacs on either side of the rectum that can cause the dog discomfort when they are full. They should empty when the dog has a bowel movement. Symptoms of inflammation or impaction are excessive licking under the tail and/or a bloody or sticky discharge from the anal area. Breeders recommend emptying the sacs on a regular schedule when bathing the dog. Many veterinarians prefer this isn't done unless there are symptoms. You can express the sacs by squeezing them (at the five and seven o'clock positions) in and up toward the anus. Take precautions not to get in the way of the foul-smelling fluid that is expressed. Some dogs object to this procedure, so it would be wise to have someone hold the head. Scooting is caused by anal-sac irritation and not worms.

Colitis

The stool may be frank blood or blood tinged and is the result of inflammation of the colon. Colitis, sometimes intermittent, can be the result of stress, undiagnosed whipworms, or perhaps idiopathic (no explainable reason). If intermittent bloody stools are an ongoing problem, you should probably feed a diet higher in fiber. Seek professional help if your dog feels poorly and/or the condition persists.

Conjunctivitis

Many breeds are prone to conjunctivitis. The conjunctiva is the pink tissue that lines the inner surface of the eyeball, except the clear, transparent cornea. Irritating substances such as bacteria, foreign matter, or chemicals can cause it to become reddened and swollen. It is important to keep any hair trimmed from around the eyes. Long hair stays damp and aggravates the problem. Keep the eyes cleaned with warm water and wipe away any matter that has accumulated in the corner of the eyes. If the condition persists, you should see your veterinarian. This problem goes hand in hand with keratoconjunctivitis sicca.

Ear Infection

Otitis externa is an inflammation of the external ear canal that begins at the outside opening of the ear and extends inward to the eardrum. Dogs with pendulous ears are prone to this disease, but breeds with upright ears also have a high incidence of problems. Allergies, food, and inhalents, along with hormonal problems, such as hypothyroidism, are major contributors to the disease. For those dogs that have recurring problems, you need to investigate the underlying causes if you hope to cure them.

Be careful never to get water in the ears. Water provides a great medium for bacteria to grow. If your dog swims or you inadvertently get water in his ears, use a drying agent. You can use an at-home preparation of equal parts of three-percent hydrogen peroxide and 70-percent rubbing alcohol. Another preparation is equal parts of white vinegar and water. Your veterinarian, alternatively, can provide a suitable product. When cleaning the ears, be careful using cotton tip applicators, because they make it easy to pack debris down into the canal. Only clean what you can see.

If your dog has an ongoing infection, don't be surprised if your veterinarian recommends sedating him and flushing his ears with a bulb syringe. Sometimes this needs to be done a few times to get the ear clean. The ear must be clean so that medication can come into contact with the canal. Be prepared to return for rechecks until the infection is gone. This may involve more flushings if the ears are very bad.

For chronic or recurring cases, your veterinarian may recommend thyroid testing, etc., and a hypoallergenic diet for a trial period of 10 to 12 weeks. Depending on your dog, it may be a good idea to see a dermatologist. Ears shouldn't be taken lightly. If the condition gets out of hand, surgery may be necessary. Please ask your veterinarian to explain proper ear maintenance for your dog.

Flea Bite Allergy

Flea bite allergy is the result of a hypersensitivity to the bite of a flea and its saliva. It only takes one bite to cause the dog to chew or scratch himself raw. Your dog may need medical attention to ease his discomfort. You need to clip the hair around the "hot spot" and wash it with a mild soap and water, and you may need to do this daily if the area weeps. Apply an antibiotic anti-inflammatory product. Hot spots can occur from other trauma, such as grooming.

Interdigital Cysts

Check for interdigital cysts on your dog's feet if he shows signs of lameness. They are frequently associated with staph infections and can be quite painful. A home remedy is to soak the infected foot in a solution of a half teaspoon of bleach in a couple of quarts of water. Do this two to three times a day for a couple of days. Check with your veterinarian for an alternative remedy; antibiotics usually work well. If there is a recurring problem, surgery may be required.

Chemicals, allergies to food and drugs, stress, and even sunburn can cause damage to your Great Pyr's skin and coat. Consult your vet if a certain condition persists.

Lameness

Lameness may only be an interdigital cyst or it could be a mat between the toes, especially if your dog licks his feet. Sometimes it is hard to determine which leg is affected. If your dog is holding up his leg, you need to see your veterinarian.

Skin

Frequently, poor skin is the result of an allergy to fleas, inhalants, or food. These types of problem usually result in a staph dermatitis. Dogs with food allergies usually show signs of severe itching and scratching. Some dogs with food allergies never

All dogs have off days when they do not seem themselves. However, if this lethargic condition persists, you should have your Great Pyrenees examined by a professional.

once itch. Their only symptom is swelling of the ears with no ear infection. Food allergy may result in recurrent bacterial skin and ear infections. Your veterinarian or dermatologist will recommend a good restricted diet. It is not wise for you to hit and miss with different dog foods. Many of the diets offered over the counter are not the hypoallergenic diet you are led to believe. Dogs acquire allergies through exposure.

Inhalant allergies result in atopy, which causes licking of the feet, scratching the body, and rubbing the muzzle. They may be seasonable. Your veterinarian or dermatologist can perform intradermal testing for inhalant allergies. If your dog should test positive, then a vaccine may be prepared. The results are very satisfying.

Tonsillitis

Usually, young dogs have a higher incidence of tonsillitis than the older ones. Older dogs have built up resistance. It is very contagious. Sometimes it is difficult to determine if the condition is tonsillitis or kennel cough because the symptoms are similar. Symptoms include fever, poor eating, swallowing with difficulty, and retching up a white, frothy mucus.

DENTAL CARE for Your Dog's Life

So, you have a new puppy! Anyone who has ever raised a puppy is abundantly aware of how this new arrival affects the household. Your puppy will chew anything he can reach, chase your shoelaces, and play "tear the rag" with any piece of clothing he can find. When puppies are newly born, they have no teeth. At about four weeks of age, puppies of most breeds begin to develop their deciduous or baby teeth. They begin eating semi-solid food, biting and fighting with their littermates, and learning discipline from their mother. As their new teeth come in, they inflict pain on their mother's breasts, so feeding sessions become less frequent and shorter. By six or eight weeks, the mother will start growling to warn her pups when they are fighting too roughly or hurting her as they nurse too much with their new teeth.

Puppies need to chew. It is a necessary part of their physical and mental development. They develop muscles and necessary life skills as they drag objects around, fight over possession, and vocalize alerts and warnings. Puppies chew on things to explore their world. They are using their sense of taste to determine what is food and what is not. How else can they tell an electrical cord from a lizard? At about four months of age, most puppies begin shedding their baby teeth. Often, these teeth need some help to come out to make way for the permanent teeth. The incisors (front teeth) will be replaced first. Then, the adult canine or fang teeth erupt. When a baby tooth is not shed before

Your dog's oral care is just as important as his grooming or nutritional needs. Developing good oral habits from the beginning of your puppy's life will keep his teeth healthy.

the permanent tooth comes in, veterinarians call it a retained deciduous tooth. This condition will often cause gum infections by trapping hair and debris between the permanent tooth and the retained baby tooth. Puppies that are given adequate chew toys will exhibit less destructive behavior, develop more physically, and have less chance of retained deciduous teeth.

During the first year, your dog should be seen by your veterinarian at regular intervals. He will let you know when to bring your puppy in for vaccinations and parasite examinations. At

Chew toys relieve your Pyr's need to chew and keep his teeth and jaw occupied.

each visit, your vet should inspect the lips, teeth, and mouth as part of a complete physical examination. You should take some part in the maintenance of your dog's oral health. Examine your dog's mouth weekly throughout his first year to make sure there are no sores, foreign objects, tooth problems, etc. If your dog drools excessively, shakes his head, or has bad breath, consult your veterinarian. By the time your dog is six months old, his permanent teeth are all in and plaque can start to accumulate on the tooth surfaces. This is when your dog needs good dental-care habits to prevent calculus buildup on his teeth. Brushing is best—that is a fact that cannot be denied. However, some dogs do not like their teeth brushed regularly, or you may not be able to accomplish the task. In this case, you should consider a product that will help prevent plaque and calculus buildup.

By the time dogs are four years old, 75 percent of them have periodontal disease. It is the most common infection in dogs.

Yearly examinations by your vet are essential to maintaining your dog's good health. If he detects periodontal disease, he or she may recommend a prophylactic cleaning. To do a thorough cleaning, it will be necessary to put your dog under anesthesia. With modern gas anesthetics and monitoring equipment, the procedure is pretty safe. Your veterinarian will scale the teeth with an ultrasound scaler or hand instrument. This removes the calculus from the teeth. If there are calculus deposits below the gum line, the veterinarian will plane the roots to make them smooth. After all of the calculus has been removed, the teeth are polished with pumice in a polishing cup. If any medical or surgical treatment is needed, it is done at this time. The final step would be fluoride treatment and your follow-up treatment at home. If the periodontal disease is advanced, the veterinarian may prescribe a medicated mouth rinse or antibiotics for use at home.

As your dog ages, professional examination and cleaning should become more frequent. The mouth should be inspected at least once a year. Your vetterinarin may recommend visits every six months. In the geriatric patient, organs such as the heart, liver, and kidneys do not function as well as when your dog was young. Your vet will probably want to test these organs' functions prior to using general anesthesia for dental cleaning. If your dog is a good chewer and you work closely with your vet, your dog can keep all of its teeth all of his life. However, as your dog ages, his sense of smell, sight, and taste will diminish. He may not have the desire to chase, trap, or chew his toys. He will also not have the energy to chew for long periods, as arthritis and periodontal disease could make chewing painful. This will leave you with more responsibility for keeping his teeth clean and healthy. The dog that would not let you brush his teeth at one year of age, may let you brush his teeth now that he is ten years old.

If you train your dog with good chewing habits as a puppy, he will have healthier teeth throughout his life.

TRAVELING with Your Dog

The earlier you start traveling with your new puppy or dog, the better. He needs to become accustomed to traveling. However, some dogs are nervous riders and become carsick easily. It is helpful if he starts any trip with an empty stomach. Do not despair, as it will go better if you continue taking him with you on short, fun rides. How would you feel if every time you rode in the car you stopped at the doctor's office for an injection? You would soon dread that nasty car. Older dogs that tend to get carsick may have more of a problem adjusting to traveling. Those dogs that are having serious problems may benefit from medication prescribed by the veterinarian.

Do give your dog a chance to relieve himself before getting into the car. It is a good idea to be prepared for a clean up with a leash, paper towels, bag, and terry cloth towel.

When in the car, the safest place for your dog is in a fiberglass or wire crate, although close confinement can promote carsickness in some dogs.

An alternative to the crate would be to use a car harness made for dogs and/or a safety strap attached to the harness or collar. Whatever you do, do not let your dog ride in the back of a pickup truck unless he is securely tied on a very short lead. I've seen trucks stop quickly, and, even though the dog was tied, he fell out and was dragged.

Another advantage of the crate is that it is a safe place to leave your dog if you need

A crate is the safest and most effective method for keeping your Great Pyrenees contained when traveling.

Never leave your dog in the car on a warm day. If your Great Pyrenees can't accompany you everywhere, leave him at home where he'll be comfortable.

to run into the store. Otherwise, you wouldn't be able to leave the windows down. Keep in mind that while many dogs are overly protective in their crates, this may not be enough to deter dognappers. In some states, it is against the law to leave a dog in the car unattended.

Never leave a dog loose in the car wearing a collar and leash. More than one dog has killed himself by hanging. Do not let him put his head out an open window. Foreign debris can be blown into his eyes. When leaving your dog unattended in a car, consider the temperature. It can take less than five minutes to reach temperatures over 100 degrees Fahrenheit.

TRIPS

Perhaps you are taking a trip. Give consideration to what is best for your dog–traveling with you or boarding. When traveling by car, van, or motor home, you need to think ahead about locking your vehicle. In all probability you have many valuables in the car and do not wish to leave it unlocked. Perhaps most valuable and not replaceable is your dog. Give thought to securing your vehicle and providing adequate ventilation for him. Another consideration for you when traveling with your dog is medical problems that may arise and little inconveniences, such as exposure to external parasites. Some areas of the country are quite flea infested. You may want to carry flea spray with you. This is even a good idea when staying in motels. Quite possibly you are not the only occupants of the room.

Unbelievably, many motels and even hotels do allow canine guests, even some very first-class ones. Gaines Pet Foods Corporation publishes *Touring With Towser*, a directory of domestic hotels and motels that accommodate guests with dogs. Their address is Gaines TWT, PO Box 5700, Kankakee, IL, 60902. Call ahead to any motel that you may be considering and see if they accept pets. Sometimes it is necessary to pay a deposit against room damage. The management may feel reassured if you mention that your dog will be crated. If you do travel with your dog, take along plenty of baggies so that you can clean up after him. When we all do our share in cleaning up, we make it possible for motels to continue accepting our pets. As a matter of fact, you should practice cleaning up everywhere you take your dog.

Depending on where your are traveling, you may need an up-to-date health certificate issued by your veterinarian. It is good policy to take along your dog's medical information, which would include the name, address, and phone number of your veterinarian, vaccination record, rabies certificate, and any medication he is taking.

AIR TRAVEL

When traveling by air, you need to contact the airlines to check their policy. Usually, you have to make arrangements up to a couple of weeks in advance when traveling with your dog. The airlines require your dog to travel in an airline approved fiberglass crate. These can be purchased through the airlines, but they are also readily available in most pet-supply stores. If your dog is not accustomed to a crate, it is a good idea to get him acclimated to it before your trip. The day

Traveling with your pet requires a lot of preparation. Before embarking on a trip, make sure that your Great Pyrenees is safe and secure when riding in a vehicle.

of the actual trip you should withhold water about one hour ahead of departure and food for about 12 hours. The airlines generally have temperature restrictions that do not allow pets to travel if it is either too cold or too hot. Frequently, these restrictions are based on the temperatures at the departure and arrival airports. It's best to inquire about a health certificate. These usually need to be issued within ten days of departure. You should arrange for nonstop, direct flights, and if a commuter plane is involved, check to see if it will carry dogs. Some don't. The Humane Society of the United States has put together a tip sheet for airline traveling. You can receive a copy by sending a self-addressed, stamped envelope to:

The Humane Society of the United States
Tip Sheet
2100 L Street NW
Washington, DC 20037.

Regulations differ for traveling outside of the country and are sometimes changed without notice. Well in advance of your trip you need to write or call the appropriate consulate or agricultural department for instructions. Some countries have lengthy quarantines (six months), and many differ in their rabies vaccination requirements. For instance, it may have to be given at least 30 days ahead of your departure.

Do make sure your dog is wearing proper identification including your name, phone number, and city. You never know when you might be in an accident and separated from your dog, or your dog could be frightened and somehow manage to escape and run away.

Another suggestion would be to carry in-case-of-emergency instructions. These would include the address and phone number of a relative or friend, your veterinarian's name, address, and phone number, and your dog's medical information.

BOARDING KENNELS

Perhaps you have decided that you need to board your dog. Your veterinarian can recommend a good boarding facility or possibly a pet sitter that will come to your house. It is customary for the boarding kennel to ask for proof of vaccination for the DHLPP, rabies, and bordetella vaccines. The bordetella should have been given within six months of boarding. This is for your protection. If they do not ask for this proof, I would not board at their kennel. Ask about flea control. Those dogs that suffer flea-bite allergy can get in trouble at a boarding kennel. Unfortunately, boarding kennels are limited as to how much they are able to do.

For more information on pet sitting, contact NAPPS:
National Association of Professional Pet Sitters
1200 G Street, NW
Suite 760
Washington, DC 20005.

Some pet clinics have technicians that pet sit and that board clinic patients in their homes. This may be an alternative for you. Ask your veterinarian if they have an employee that can help you. There is a definite advantage to having a technician care for your dog, especially if he is on medication or is a senior citizen.

You can write to the ASPCA for a copy of *Traveling With Your Pet:* ASPCA, Education Department, 441 E. 92nd Street, New York, NY 10128.

IDENTIFICATION and Finding the Lost Dog

There are several ways of identifying your dog. The old standby is a collar with dog license, rabies, and ID tags. Unfortunately, collars have a way of being separated from dogs and tags fall off. We're not suggesting you shouldn't use a collar and tags. If they stay intact and on the dog, they are the quickest form of identification.

For several years, owners have been tattooing their dogs. Some tattoos use a number with a registry. Herein lies the problem, because there are several registries to check. If you wish to tattoo your dog, use your social security number. Humane shelters have the means to trace it. It is usually done on the inside of the rear thigh. The area is first shaved and numbed. There is no pain, although some dogs do not like the buzzing sound. Occasionally, tattooing is not legible and needs to be redone.

The newest method of identification is microchipping. The microchip is a computer chip that is no larger than a grain of rice. The veterinarian implants it by injection between the shoulder blades. The dog feels no discomfort. If your dog is lost and picked up by the humane society, they can trace you by scanning the

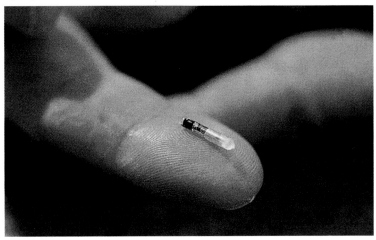

The newest method of identification is the microchip, which is a computer chip no bigger than a grain of rice that can help you track your dog's whereabouts.

136

Your Great Pyrenees should wear his collar and ID tags at all times in case he becomes separated from you.

microchip, which has its own code. Most microchip scanners are friendly to other brands of microchips and their registries. The microchip comes with a dog tag saying that the dog is microchipped. It is the safest way of identifying your dog.

FINDING THE LOST DOG
Most people would agree that there would be little worse than losing your dog. Responsible pet owners rarely lose their dogs. They do not let their dogs run free because they don't want harm to come to them. Not only that, but in most, if not all, states there is a leash law.

Beware of fenced-in yards. They can be a hazard. Dogs find ways to escape either over or under fences. Another fast exit may be through the gate that perhaps someone left unlocked.

Below is a list that will hopefully be of help to you if you lose your pet. Remember, don't give up, keep looking. Your dog is worth your efforts.

1. Contact your neighbors and put flyers with a photo on it in their mailboxes. Information you should include would be the dog's name, breed, sex, color, age, source of identification, when your dog was last seen and where, and your name and phone numbers. It may be helpful to say that the dog needs medical care. Offer a *reward*.

2. Check all local shelters daily. It is also possible for your dog to be picked up away from home and end up in an out-of-the-way shelter. Check these, too. Go in person. It is not enough to call. Most shelters are limited on the time they can hold dogs before they are put up for adoption or euthanized. There is the possibility that your dog will not make it to the shelter for several days. He could have been wandering or someone may have tried to keep him.

3. Notify all local veterinarians. Call and send flyers.
4. Call your breeder. Frequently, breeders are contacted when one of their breed is found.
5. Contact the rescue group for your breed.
6. Contact local schools—children may have seen your dog.
7. Post flyers at the schools, groceries, gas stations, convenience stores, veterinary clinics, groomers, and any other places that will allow them.
8. Advertise in the newspaper.
9. Advertise on the radio.

BEHAVIOR and Canine Communication

S
tudies of the human/animal bond point out the importance of the unique relationships that exist between people and their pets. Those of us who share our lives with pets understand the special part they play through companionship, service, and protection. For many, the pet/owner bond goes beyond simple companionship; pets are often considered members of the family. A leading pet food manufacturer recently conducted a nationwide survey of pet owners to gauge just how important pets were in their lives. Here's what they found:

· 76 percent allow their pets to sleep on their beds
· 78 percent think of their pets as their children
· 84 percent display photos of their pets, mostly in their homes
· 84 percent think that their pets react to their own emotions
· 100 percent talk to their pets
· 97 percent think that their pets understand what they're saying
Are you surprised?

Senior citizens show more concern for their own eating habits when they have the responsibility of feeding a dog. Seeing that their dogs are routinely exercised encourages the owners to think of schedules that otherwise may seem unimportant to a senior citizen. The older owner may be arthritic and feeling poorly, but with responsibility for his dog he has a reason to get up and get moving. It is a big plus if his dog is an attention seeker that will demand such from his owner.

Over the last couple of decades, it has been shown that pets relieve the stress of those who lead busy lives. Owning a pet has been known to lessen the occurrence of heart attack and stroke.

Many single folks thrive on the companionship of their dogs. Lifestyles are very different from a long time ago, and today more individuals seek the single life. However, they receive fulfillment from owning dogs.

Most likely, the majority of our dogs live in family environments. The companionship they provide is well worth the effort involved. In my opinion, every child should have the opportunity to have a family dog. Dogs teach responsibility through the understanding of their care, feelings, and even respect for their life cycles. Frequently, those children who have not been exposed to dogs

Having your child take part in caring for the family dog is a good lesson in responsibility. It also helps a child to feel comfortable and secure around animals.

grow up afraid of them, which isn't good. Dogs sense timidity, and some will take advantage of the situation.

Today, more dogs are working as service dogs. Since the origination of the Seeing Eye dogs years ago, we now have dogs trained to aid the deaf. Also, dogs are trained to provide service for the handicapped and are able to perform many different tasks for their owners. Search and rescue dogs, with their handlers, are sent throughout the world to assist in the recovery of disaster victims. They are lifesavers.

Therapy dogs are very popular with nursing homes, and some hospitals even allow them to visit. The inhabitants truly look forward to their visits. They wanted and were allowed to have visiting dogs to hold and love.

Nationally, there is a Pet Awareness Week to educate students and others about the value and basic care of our pets. Many countries take an even greater interest in their pets than Americans do. In those countries, pets are allowed to accompany their owners into restaurants and shops, etc. In the US, this freedom is only available to our service dogs. Even so, we think very highly of the human/animal bond.

CANINE BEHAVIOR

Canine behavior problems are the number-one reason that pet owners dispose of their dogs, either through new homes, humane shelters, or euthanasia. Unfortunately, there are too many owners who are unwilling to devote the necessary time to properly train their dogs. On the other hand, there are those who are not only concerned about inherited health problems but are also aware of the dog's mental stability.

You may realize that a breed and his group relatives (i.e., sporting, hounds, etc.) show tendencies toward behavioral characteristics. An experienced breeder can acquaint you with his breed's personality. Unfortunately, many breeds are labeled with poor temperaments, when actually the breed as a whole is not affected but rather only a small percentage of individuals within the breed.

Inheritance and environment contribute to the dog's behavior. Some naïve people suggest inbreeding as the cause of bad temperaments. Inbreeding only results in poor behavior if the ancestors carry the trait. If there are excellent temperaments behind the dogs, then good breeding practices will promote good temperaments in the offspring. Did you ever consider that inbreeding is what sets the characteristics of a breed? A purebred dog is the end result of inbreeding. This does not spare the mixed-breed dog from the same problems. Mixed-breed dogs are frequently the offspring of purebred dogs.

Not too many decades ago most dogs led a different lifestyle than what is prevalent today. Usually, mom stayed home so the dog had human companionship and someone to discipline

Pets need to feel like they are an integral part of their families' lives. Do your best to provide a loving and stimulating environment for your Great Pyrenees.

141

him if needed. Not much was expected from the family pet. Today's mom works, and everyone's life is at a much faster pace. The dog may have to adjust to being a "weekend" dog. The family is gone all day during the week and he is left to his own devices for entertainment. Some dogs sleep all day waiting for their families to come home, and others become wigwam wreckers if given the opportunity. Crates do ensure the safety of the dog and the house. However, he could become physically and emotionally crippled if he doesn't get enough exercise and attention. We still appreciate and want the companionship of our dogs, although we expect more from them. In many cases, we tend to forget dogs are just that—*dogs* not human beings.

SOCIALIZING AND TRAINING

Many prospective puppy buyers lack experience regarding the proper socialization and training needed to develop the type of pets we all desire. In the first 18 months, training does take some work. It is easier to start proper training before there is a problem that needs to be corrected.

Introducing your Great Pyrenees to new people, places, and experiences will help your puppy to become a confident and well-socialized adult.

Breeders usually begin socializing their puppies at five to six weeks of age. It's vital to your pup's well-being that you continue this socialization process.

The initial work begins with the breeder. The breeder should start socializing the puppy at five to six weeks of age and cannot let up. Human socializing is critical up through 12 weeks of age and is likewise important during the following months. The litter should be left together during the first few weeks, but it is necessary to separate the pups by ten weeks of age. Leaving them together after that time will increase competition for litter dominance. If puppies are not socialized with people by 12 weeks of age, they will be timid in later life.

The eight- to ten-week age period is a fearful time for puppies. They need to be handled very gently by children and adults. There should be no harsh discipline during this time. Starting at 14 weeks of age, the puppy begins the juvenile period, which ends when he reaches sexual maturity around 6 to 14 months of age. During the juvenile period, he needs to be introduced to strangers (adults, children, and other dogs) on the home property. At sexual maturity, he will begin to bark at strangers and become more protective. Males start to lift their legs to urinate, but you can inhibit this behavior by walking your boy on leash away from trees, shrubs, fences, etc.

Perhaps you are thinking about getting an older puppy. You need to inquire about the puppy's social experience. If he has lived in a kennel, he may have a hard time adjusting to people and environmental stimuli. Assuming he has had a good social upbringing, there are advantages to an older puppy.

Training includes puppy kindergarten and a minimum of one to two basic training classes. During these classes, you will learn how to train your youngster. This is especially important if you own a large breed of dog. It is somewhat harder, if not nearly impossible, for some owners to be the alpha figure when their dog reaches adult size. You will be taught how to properly restrain your dog. This concept is important. Again, it puts you in the alpha position. All dogs need to be restrained many times during their lives. Believe it or not, some of the worst offenders are the eight-week-old puppies that are brought to our clinic. They need to be gently restrained for a nail trim, but the way they carry on you would think we were killing them. In comparison, their vaccination is a "piece of cake." When we ask dogs to do something that is not agreeable to them, their worst comes out. Life will be easier for your dog if you expose him at a young age to the necessities of life—proper behavior and restraint.

Understanding the Dog's Language

Most authorities agree that the dog is a descendent of the wolf. The dog and wolf have similar traits. For instance both are pack oriented and prefer not to be isolated for long periods of time. Another characteristic is that the dog, like the wolf, looks to the leader—alpha—for direction. Both the wolf and the dog communicate through body language, not only within their packs but with outsiders.

Every pack has an alpha figure. The dog looks to you, or should look to you, to be that leader. If your dog doesn't receive the proper training and guidance, he very well may replace you as alpha. This would be a serious problem and is certainly a disservice to your dog.

Eye contact is one way the alpha wolf keeps order within his pack. You are alpha so you must establish eye contact with your puppy. Obviously, your puppy will have to look at you. Practice eye contact, even if you need to hold his head for five to ten seconds at a time. You can give him a treat as a reward. Make sure your eye contact is gentle and not threatening. Later, if he has been naughty, it is permissible to give him a long, penetrating look. There are some older dogs that never learned eye contact as

Learning how a dog communicates will help you to better understand certain behaviors.

145

If your dog is acting fearful of a situation or object, don't dwell on his fright. Instead, direct his attention on to something else.

puppies and cannot accept eye contact. You should avoid eye contact with these dogs since they feel threatened and will retaliate as such.

BODY LANGUAGE
The play bow, when the forequarters are down and the hindquarters are elevated, is an invitation to play. Puppies play fight, which helps them learn the acceptable limits of biting. This is necessary later in their lives. Nevertheless, an owner may be falsely reassured by the playful nature of his dog's aggression. Playful aggression toward another dog or human may be an indication of serious aggression in the future. Owners should never play fight or play tug-of-war with any dog that is inclined to be dominant.

Signs of submission are:
1. Avoids eye contact.
2. Active submission–the dog crouches down, ears back and tail lowered.
3. Passive submission–the dog rolls on his side, with his hindlegs in the air, and frequently urinates.

Signs of dominance are:
1. Makes eye contact.
2. Stands with ears up, tail up, and the hair raised on his neck.
3. Shows dominance over another dog by standing at right angles over him.

Dominant dogs tend to behave in characteristic ways such as:
1. The dog may be unwilling to move from his place (i.e., reluctant to give up the sofa if the owner wants to sit there).

2. He may not part with toys or objects in his mouth and may show possessiveness with his food bowl.
3. He may not respond quickly to commands.
4. He may be disagreeable for grooming and dislikes being petted.

Dogs are popular because of their sociable nature. Those that have contact with humans during the first 12 weeks of life regard them as a member of their own species—their pack. All dogs have the potential for both dominant and submissive behavior. Only through experience and training do they learn to whom it is appropriate to show which behavior. Not all dogs are concerned with dominance, but owners need to be aware of that potential. It is wise for the owner to establish his dominance early on.

A human can express dominance or submission toward a dog in the following ways:
1. Meeting the dog's gaze signals dominance. Averting the gaze signals submission. If the dog growls or threatens, averting the gaze is the first avoiding action to take—it may prevent attack. It is important to establish eye contact in the puppy. The older dog that has not been exposed to eye

Dogs that have been socialized with humans at an early age regard them as members of their own species or pack.

147

contact may see it as a threat and will not be willing to submit.
2. Being above the dog signals dominance; being lower
signals submission. This is why, when attempting to make
friends with a strange dog or catch the runaway, one should
kneel down to his level. Some owners see their dogs become
dominant when allowed on the furniture or on the bed. Then
the dog is at the owner's level.
3. An owner can gain dominance by ignoring all the dog's
social initiatives. The owner pays attention to the dog only
when he obeys a command.

No dog should be allowed to achieve dominant status over any
adult or child. Ways of preventing this are as follows:
1. Handle the puppy gently, especially during the three- to
four-month period.
2. Let the children and adults handfeed him and teach him
to take food without lunging or grabbing.
3. Do not allow him to chase children or joggers.
4. Do not allow him to jump on people or mount their legs.
Even females may be inclined to mount. It is not only a male
habit.
5. Do not allow him to growl for any reason.
6. Don't participate in wrestling or tug-of-war games.
7. Don't physically punish a puppy for aggressive behavior.
Restrain him from repeating the infraction and teach an
alternative behavior. Dogs should earn everything they receive
from their owners. This would include sitting to receive
petting or treats, sitting before going out the door, and sitting
to receive the collar and leash. These types of exercise
reinforce the owner's dominance.

Young children should never be left alone with a dog. It is
important that children learn some basic obedience commands
so they have some control over the dog. They will gain his
respect.

Fear

One of the most common problems dogs can experience is
being fearful. Some dogs are more afraid than others. On the lesser
side, which is sometimes humorous to watch, dogs can be afraid
of a strange object. They act silly when something is out of place
in the house. We call his problem perceptive intelligence. He
realizes the abnormal within his known environment. He does

If your dog is behaving aggressively, have him perform a simple command, like the sit, which immediately puts you in a dominant position.

not react the same way in strange environments since he does not know what is normal.

On the more serious side is a fear of people. This can result in backing off, seeking his own space and saying "leave me alone" or it can result in an aggressive behavior that may lead to challenging the person. Respect that the dog wants to be left alone and give him time to come forward. If you approach the cornered dog, he may resort to snapping. If you leave him alone, he may decide to come forward, which should be rewarded with a treat.

Some dogs may initially be too fearful to take treats. In these cases it is helpful to make sure the dog hasn't eaten for about 24 hours. Being a little hungry encourages him to accept the treats, especially if they are of the "gourmet" variety.

Dogs can be afraid of numerous things, including loud noises and thunderstorms. Invariably, the owner rewards (by comforting) the dog when he shows signs of fearfulness. When your dog is frightened, direct his attention to something else. Don't dwell on his fright.

Aggression

Some different types of aggression are: predatory, defensive, dominance, possessive, protective, fear induced, noise provoked, "rage" syndrome (unprovoked aggression), maternal, and aggression directed toward other dogs. Aggression is the most common behavioral problem encountered. Protective breeds are expected to be more aggressive than others, but with the proper upbringing they can make very dependable companions. You need to be able to read your dog.

Many factors contribute to aggression, including genetics and environment. An improper environment, which may include living conditions, lack of social life, excessive punishment, being attacked or frightened by an aggressive dog, etc., can all influence a dog's behavior. Even spoiling him and giving too much praise may be detrimental. Isolation and the lack of human contact or exposure to frequent teasing by children or adults also can ruin a good dog.

Lack of direction, fear, or confusion lead to aggression in those dogs that are so inclined. Any obedience exercise, even the sit and down, can direct the dog and overcome his fear and/or confusion. Every dog should learn these commands as a youngster, and there should be periodic reinforcement.

All Items Out

Sussex Wantage Library
05/08/09 02:27PM
973-875-3940

PATRON: CASTRO, MARY ROSE
***
NEW OWNERS GUIDE TO PYRENEES
CALL NO: FAST ADD
DUE DATE: 05/29/09

GREAT PYRENEES
CALL NO: FAST ADD
DUE DATE: 05/29/09

TOTAL ITEMS OUT: 2

Renew online @
www.sussexcountylibrary.org

When a dog is showing signs of aggression, you should speak calmly (no screaming or hysterics) and firmly give a command that he understands, such as the sit. As soon as your dog obeys, you have assumed your dominant position. Aggression presents a problem because there may be danger to others. Sometimes it is an emotional issue. Owners may consciously or unconsciously encourage their dogs' aggression. Other owners show responsibility by accepting the problem and taking measures to keep it under control. The owner is responsible for his dog's actions, and it is not wise to take a chance on someone being bitten, especially a child. Euthanasia is the solution for some owners, and in severe cases this may be the best choice. However, few dogs are that dangerous and very few are that much of a threat to their owners. If caution is exercised and professional help is gained early on, most cases can be controlled.

Some authorities recommend feeding a lower protein (less than 20 percent) diet. They believe this can aid in reducing aggression. If the dog loses weight, vegetable oil can be added. Veterinarians and behaviorists are having some success with pharmacology. In many cases, treatment is possible and can improve the situation.

If you have done everything according to "the book" regarding training and socializing and are still having a behavior problem, don't procrastinate. It is important that the problem gets attention before it is out of hand. It is estimated that 20 percent of a veterinarian's time may be devoted to dealing with problems before they become so intolerable that the dog is separated from his home and owner. If your veterinarian isn't able to help, he should refer you to a behaviorist.

PROBLEMS

Barking

Barking is a habit that shouldn't be encouraged. Some owners desire their dogs to bark so as to be watchdogs. Most dogs will bark when a stranger comes to the door.

The new puppy frequently barks or whines in the crate in his strange, unfamiliar environment, and the owner reinforces the puppy's bad behavior by going to him during the night. This is a no-no. Smack the top of the crate and say, "Quiet," in a loud, firm voice. Puppies don't like to hear the loud noise of a crate being banged. If the barking is sleep-interrupting, the owner should take crate and pup to the bedroom for a few days until the puppy becomes adjusted to his new environment. Otherwise, ignore the barking during the night.

Barking can be a breed trait or a bad habit learned through the environment. It takes dedication to stop the barking. Attention should be paid to the cause of it. Does the dog seek attention, does he need to go out, is it feeding time, is it occurring when he is left alone, is it a protective bark, etc.? Overzealous barking can be a breed tendency. When barking presents a problem for you, try to stop it as soon as it begins.

There are electronic collars available that are supposed to curb barking. There are some disadvantages to the collar. If the dog is barking out of excitement, punishment is not the appropriate treatment. Presumably, there is the chance the collar could be activated by other stimuli and thereby punish the dog when he is not barking. If you decide to use one, you should seek help from a person with experience with that type of collar. Nevertheless, the root of the problem needs to be investigated and corrected.

In extreme circumstances (usually when there is a problem with the neighbors), some people have resorted to having their dogs debarked. Be cautioned that the dog continues to bark, but usually only a squeaking sound is heard. Frequently, the vocal cords grow back. Probably the biggest concern is that the dog can be left with scar tissue, which can narrow the opening to the trachea.

Jumping Up

A dog that jumps up is a happy dog. Nevertheless, few guests appreciate dogs jumping on them. Clothes get footprinted and/or snagged.

Some trainers believe in allowing the puppy to jump up during his first few weeks. If you correct him too soon and at the wrong age, you may intimidate him. Consequently, he could be timid around humans later in his life. However, there will come a time, probably around four months of age, that he needs to know when it is okay to jump and when he is to show off good manners by sitting instead.

Some authorities never allow jumping. If you are irritated by your dog jumping up on you, then you should discourage it from

Dogs usually jump when they are excited and happy. However, a large breed of dog like the Great Pyrenees could cause harm to a small child or an elderly person. Firmly tell your dog, "No" when he jumps up.

the beginning. A larger breed of dog can cause harm to a senior citizen. Some are quite fragile. It may not take much to cause a topple that could break a hip.

How do you correct the problem? All family members need to participate in teaching the puppy to sit as soon as he starts to jump up. The sit must be practiced every time he does it. Don't forget to praise him for his good behavior. If an older dog has acquired the habit, grasp his paws and squeeze tightly. Give a firm "No." He'll soon catch on. Remember the entire family must take part. Each time you allow him to jump up you go back a step in training.

Biting

All puppies bite and try to chew on your fingers, toes, arms, etc. This is the time to teach them to be gentle and not to bite hard. Put your fingers in your puppy's mouth and if he bites too hard then say "easy" and let him know he's hurting you. Squeal and act like you have been seriously hurt. If the puppy plays too rough and doesn't respond to your corrections, then he needs "time out" in his crate. You should be particularly careful with young children and puppies that still have their deciduous (baby) teeth. Those teeth are like needles and can leave little scars on youngsters.

Biting in the more mature dog is something that should be prevented at all costs. If it occurs,s quickly let him know in no uncertain terms that biting will not be tolerated. When biting is directed toward another dog (dog fight), don't get in the middle of it. Some authorities recommend breaking up a fight by elevating the hind legs. This would only be possible if there was a person to handle each dog. Obviously, it would be hard to fight with the hind legs off the ground. A dog bite is serious and should be given attention. Wash the bite with soap and water and contact your doctor. It is important to know the status of the offender's rabies vaccination.

Your dog must know who is boss. When biting occurs, you should seek professional help at once. On the other hand, you must not let your dog intimidate you and be so afraid of a bite that you can't discipline him. Professional help through your veterinarian, dog trainer, and/or behaviorist can give you guidance.

Digging

Bored dogs release their frustrations through mischievous behavior such as digging. Dogs shouldn't be left unattended outside, even if they are in a fenced-in yard. Usually, the dog is sent to "jail" (the backyard) because the owner can't tolerate him in the house. The culprit feels socially deprived and needs to be included in the owner's life. The owner has neglected the dog's training. The dog has not developed into the companion we desire. If you are one of these owners, then perhaps it is possible for you to change. Give him another chance. Some owners object to their dogs' unkempt coat and doggy odor. See that he is groomed on a regular schedule and look into some training classes.

Submissive Urination

Submissive urination is not a housetraining problem. It can occur in all breeds and may be more prevalent in some. Usually, it occurs in puppies, but occasionally it occurs in older dogs and may be in response to physical praise. Try verbal praise or ignoring your dog until after he has had a chance to relieve himself. Scolding will only make the problem worse. Many dogs outgrow this problem.

Coprophagia

Also know as stool eating, coprophagia sometimes occurs without a cause. It may begin with boredom and then becomes a habit that is hard to break. Your best remedy is to keep the puppy on a leash and keep the yard picked up, so he won't have an opportunity to get into trouble. Your veterinarian can dispense a medication that is put on the dog's food that makes the stool taste bitter. Of course, this will do little good if your dog cleans up after other dogs.

Food Guarding

If you see signs of your puppy guarding his food, you should take immediate steps to correct the problem. It is not fair to your

Puppies and even adult dogs can get into mischief if they are bored. Provide your Great Pyrenees with enough physical activity to prevent him from getting into trouble.

puppy to feed him in a busy environment where children or other pets may interfere with his eating. This can be the cause of food guarding. Puppies should be fed in their crates where they do not feel threatened. Another advantage of this is that the puppy gets down to the business of eating and doesn't fool around. Perhaps you have seen possessiveness over the food bowl or his toys. Start by feeding him out of your hand, and teach him that it is okay for you to remove his food bowl or toys and that you most assuredly will return them to him. If your dog is truly a bad actor and intimidates you, try keeping him on leash and perhaps sit next to him making happy talk. At feeding time, make him work for his reward (his dinner) by doing some obedience command such as sit or down. Before your problem gets out of control, you should get professional help. If he is out of control over toys, perhaps you should dispose of them or at least put them away when young children are around.

Mischief and Misbehavior

All puppies and even some adult dogs will get into mischief at some time in their lives. You should start by "puppy proofing" your house. Even so, it is impossible to have a sterile environment. For instance, if you would be down to four walls and a floor, your dog could still chew a hole in the wall. What do you do? Remember puppies should never be left unsupervised, so let us go on to the trusted adult dog that has misbehaved. His behavior may be an attention getter. Dogs, and even children, are known to do mischief even though they know they will be punished. Your puppy/dog will benefit from more attention and new direction. He may benefit from a training class or by reinforcement of the obedience he has already learned. How about a daily walk? That could be a good outlet for your dog, time together, and exercise for both of you.

Separation Anxiety

Separation anxiety occurs when dogs feel distress or apprehension about being separated from their owners. One of the mistakes owners make is to set their dogs up for their departure. Some authorities recommend paying little attention to the pet for at least ten minutes before leaving, and for the first ten minutes after you arrive home. The dog isn't cued to the fact you are leaving, and if you keep it low key, he learns to accept it as a

If your dog is having anxiety about being left alone, try leaving him for just a few minutes at a time, then returning and rewarding him with a treat.

normal everyday occurrence. Those dogs that are used to being crated usually accept your departure. Dogs that are anxious may have a serious problem and wreak havoc on the house within a few minutes after your departure. You can try to acclimate your dog to the separation by leaving for just a few minutes at a time, and returning and rewarding him with a treat. Don't get too carried away. Plan on this process taking a long time. A behaviorist can set down a schedule for you. Those dogs that are insecure, such as ones obtained from a humane shelter or those that have changed homes, may present more of a problem.

Punishment

A puppy should learn that correction is sometimes necessary and should not question your authority. An older dog that has never received correction may retaliate. There may be a time for physical punishment, but this does not mean hitting the dog. Do not use newspapers, fly swatters, etc. One type of correction that is used by the mother dog when she corrects her puppies is to take the puppy by the scruff and shake him *gently*. For the older, larger dog, you can grab the scruff, one hand on each side of his neck, and lift his legs off the ground. This is effective because dogs feel intimidated when their feet are off the ground. Timing is of the utmost importance when punishment is necessary. Depending on the degree of fault, you might want to reinforce punishment by ignoring your dog for 15 to 20 minutes. Whatever you do, do not overdo corrections or they will lose value.

The most important advice to you is to be aware of your dog's actions. Even so, remember dogs are dogs and will behave as such, even though we might like them to be perfect little people. You and your dog will become neurotic if you worry about every little indiscretion. When there is reason for concern—don't waste time. Seek guidance. Dogs are meant to be loved and enjoyed.

REFERENCES
Manual of Canine Behavior. Valerie O'Farrell. British Small Animal Veterinary Association.
Good Owners, Great Dogs. Brian Kilcommons, Warner Books.

INDEX

PHOTO CREDITS

Ruth Baak, 15, 62, 106
Stephan and Mary Berman, 18, 30, 33, 39, 44, 57, 58, 59, 70, 78, 84, 94
Mary Fodness, 127, 157
Isabelle Francais, 8, 21, 31, 37, 47 48, 52, 55, 56, 65, 67, 68, 69, 71, 73, 74, 77, 79, 80, 83, 86, 87, 88, 89, 92, 93, 97, 99, 102, 108, 111, 114, 117, 119, 121, 122, 128, 129, 131, 140, 146, 155
Kim Lasley, 12, 17, 19, 23, 25, 26, 27, 28, 29, 32, 35, 43, 50, 51, 61, 64, 109, 126, 134, 141, 142, 143, 145, 147, 149, 153
Christine Palmer-Persen, 11, 41, 45, 60, 81, 115, 118, 132
Kristina Sodeika-Trinka, 101